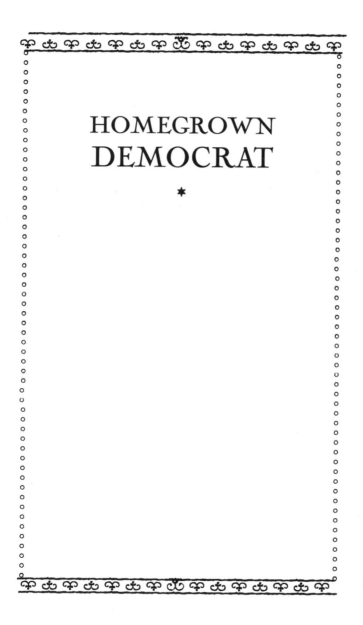

HOMEGROWN
DEMOCRAT

★

HOMEGROWN DEMOCRAT

A Few Plain Thoughts from the
Heart of America

GARRISON KEILLOR

* * *
*

VIKING

VIKING

Published by the Penguin Group

Penguin Group (USA) Inc., 375 Hudson Street, New York, New York 10014, U.S.A.

Penguin Books Ltd, 80 Strand, London WC2R 0RL, England

Penguin Books Australia Ltd, 250 Camberwell Road, Camberwell, Victoria 3124, Australia

Penguin Books Canada Ltd, 10 Alcorn Avenue, Toronto, Ontario, Canada M4V 3B2

Penguin Books India (P) Ltd, 11 Community Centre, Panchsheel Park, New Delhi – 110 017, India

Penguin Group (NZ), Cnr Airborne and Rosedale Roads, Albany, Auckland 1310, New Zealand

Penguin Books (South Africa) (Pty) Ltd, 24 Sturdee Avenue, Rosebank, Johannesburg 2196, South Africa

Penguin Books Ltd, Registered Offices:
80 Strand, London WC2R 0RL, England

First published in 2004 by Viking Penguin,
a member of Penguin Group (USA) Inc.

10 9 8 7 6 5 4 3 2

LIBRARY OF CONGRESS CATALOGING IN PUBLICATION DATA

Keillor, Garrison.
    Homegrown democrat / Garrison, Kellor.
        p. cm.
    ISBN 0-670-03365-0
    1. Democracy—United States.   2. United States—Politics and government.
3. Keillor, Garrison.   4. Authors, American—20th century—Biography.   5. Radio
broadcasters—United States—Biography.   6. Democratic Party (U.S.)
7. Republican Party (U.S. : 1854–)   8. United States—Economic policy.   9. United
States—Social policy.   10 Minnesota—Social conditions.   I. Title.

JK1726.K37   2004
320.973—dc22   2004053565

This book is printed on acid-free paper. ∞

Printed in the United States of America
Set in Aldus
Designed by Carla Bolte

TO ALL OF THE
GOOD DEMOCRATIC-FARMER-LABORITES
OF MINNESOTA

CONTENTS

DON'T

THINK ILL

of

DEMOCRATS,

YOU MAY BE

ONE OF US.

* * *

*

HOMEGROWN
DEMOCRAT

Chapter 1

DON'T THINK
YOU'RE SPECIAL

There was a young man from the City
Who formed a Campaign Committee
But gave up the race
When he saw that his face
Looked just like his butt—what a pity.

I AM A Democrat, which was nothing I decided for myself but simply the way I was brought up, starting
with the idea of *Do unto others as you would have them
do unto you,* which is the basis of the simple social compact by which we live and also *You are not so different
from other people so don't give yourself airs,* which was
drummed into us children back in the old days when
everyone went to public schools. Don't be conceited. So
you can write: goody-goody for you, but don't think

1

you're a genius because, believe me, you're not. The democracy of the gospel. *All have sinned and come short of the glory of God. All we like sheep have gone astray.* These articles of faith, plus our common tongue and a fondness for jokes and the American landscape, bind us together in a union of souls, each one free, each one devoted to the union.

These things were not so clear to me when I was young and immortal, but now I am part of the democracy of old age, impressed on me in 2001 when my mitral valve came loose and I was wheeled into a bright blue industrial room at Mayo and masked and eight hours later my little boat bumped up on a foggy shore and a young woman named Erinn said I would be okay and the next day my catheter was removed and that night a nurse in a blue uniform with a pager clipped to her lapel bent down to take my blood pressure and the weight of the pager opened the fabulous landscape of her breasts and my libido awakened, but I digress. I grew up among Bible-believing people in Minnesota, a cold weather state when the jet stream slips and the wind blows steadily from Manitoba; it gets so cold your skin hurts, your innards clench up, and a man's testes shrink to the size of garden peas, but—*Everyone else is just as cold as you are so don't complain about it, this is not a personal experience,* that's what we say, and you comfort yourself with fried eggs and bacon and you bulk up a good deal by spring, but then everyone else is fat too, so it's not a problem.

Here we have the democracy of flatness: there simply aren't so many hills for rich people to live on top of. We suffer less from the self-esteem issues that make people call on their cell phones and announce their whereabouts. There was no radio in *The Spirit of St. Louis* and nobody knew where Lindbergh was as he flew the Atlantic until some fishermen spotted him off the Irish coast, but a man on a train from New York to Boston must furnish frequent updates on his progress. In Minnesota, we get home when we get home, no big deal. And if we're caught in traffic and miss the sales meeting, it won't matter that much in the end. The marketing of widgets will go on, our impact on the world is slight, so take life as a comedy and play it for laughs. You die, there is a sort of decent grief and a few people really do suffer from your absence, but the impact on the greater world is negligible. You do not leave a big hole. They dig a hole and put you in it.

The state was settled by no-nonsense socialists from Germany and Sweden and Norway who unpacked their trunks and planted corn and set about organizing schools; churches; libraries; lodges; societies and benevolent associations; brotherhoods and sisterhoods, and raised their children to Mind Your Manners, Be Useful, Pay Attention, Make Something of Yourself, Turn Down the Thermostat (If You're Cold, Go Put on a Sweater), Share and Share Alike, Be Satisfied with What You Have—a green Jell-O salad with mandarin oranges, miniature marshmallows, walnuts, and Miracle Whip is by God good enough for anybody. I grew up in the pure democracy of a public grade school where everybody brought a valentine for everybody on Valentine's Day so we should feel equally loved though of course some valentines are more equal than others, some have lace and little flaps under which special endearments are written, and others are generic, printed six to a page with bumpy edges where they were torn on the dotted line. But you should be happy with what you get and Don't Think You're Special Because You're Not. (Those people on daytime TV talking about how their parents never gave them the positive feedback they needed and that's why they shot them—those are not Minnesotans. Nor are the people who go to court to win their children the right to not say the Pledge of Allegiance or not be in the room when other children are saying it.) We take pains to not be Special. If there is one meatball left on the platter, you do not take it, you take half of it, and someone else takes half of that and so it is endlessly divided down to the last crumb. Not a state of showboats or motormouths. We tend not to be uncomfortable about silence and can sit in the company of others and eat and not a word is said and it's okay by us. *Silence, the purest democracy.* The sweetest part of Sunday morning: when the organ stops and nobody speaks and we look at the light streaming in the windows.

I live in Minnesota for the plain and simple reason that *I am not so different from these people* and also because the social compact is still intact here, despite Republicans trying to pound it out of us.

Here in St. Paul, I live a few blocks from where my mother lived back in the Dirty Thirties when she was a slim, shy, lovely teenager attending St. Paul Central and hoping to become a registered nurse and earning her keep by going door-to-door in the neighborhood selling freshly baked peanut-butter cookies in little brown paper bags. It's also the neighborhood of F. Scott Fitzgerald's boyhood, who wrote plays and got his chums to perform them, with himself in the starring role. For all that's changed since then, a good deal has not—people still say Please and Excuse me and Good morning and hold the door open for you and indulge the free spirits among us though it's irksome when their dandelions go to seed and blow onto our land. If you're in the mood, you can make small talk with us and we will make small talk back. The art of small talk is beautiful and intricate and hard for foreigners to learn. It does not preclude large talk. You could be waiting for the Grand Avenue bus with a man you've seen around the neighborhood over the years, at the dry cleaner's and Kowalski's and Tom the Tailor's and La Cucaracha and ask him how he's doing and he'll tell you about the death of his father in the hospital the night before and you will listen to his spontaneous monologue and ease his loneliness a little. An utterly common occurrence in a society that isn't hung up on social status—people turning to each other and dishing up a story of astonishing frankness and intimacy.

In the new privatized low-tax minimal-services society the Republicans are striving to lay on us, public transportation will offer no pleasure whatsoever. The bus will be for losers and dopes. The driver will sit in a bulletproof box and there will be no conversation with him. The bus will be full of angry and sullen people who have lost hope that their kids can rise in the world and have a better life, which is the hope that makes it possible for me to turn to you and say something about the weather. Civility leads to civilities. In Republican America, you will not enjoy public life *period*. The public library, that great democratic temple, will become a waiting room for desperate and broken people, the alkies, the wacked-out, the unemployables, and the public schools will become holding tanks for children whose parents were too unresourceful to find good schools for them, and politics will be so ugly and rancid that decent people will avoid expressing an opinion for fear of being screeched at and hectored and spat on.

That isn't the country I grew up in, dear hearts.

I grew up in a sweet country that was one country and so there were certain points where all roads led and everybody came together, nabob and yahoo, poet and redneck, Baptist and Catholic, and the public school was one of those places. In Anoka, Minnesota, some children wound up attending Dartmouth and Stanford and Carleton and Princeton but they spent their formative years in the public school system with the children of farmers and carpenters and cops and firemen. They all rode together on the big yellow schoolbus and cheered for the Tornadoes and ate macaroni and cheese in the lunchroom. This experience is valuable. It gives you a tribal feeling. Everybody else knows the same songs you do, including *Nobody likes me, everybody hates me, guess I'll go eat worms* and *Did you ever think as the hearse rolls by that you may be the next to die?* And the one about the doctor and the nurse and the lady with the alligator purse. And *Minnesota, hats off to thee, to your colors true we shall ever be* and maybe *All Glory Laud and Honor to Thee O Saviour King, to Whom the Lips of Children Made Sweet Hosannas Ring*—or maybe not, there's room for diversity here—but we all grew up on the same playground and skipped rope to *Mable, Mable, set the table, she put on the red hot pepper* and played Rover Red Rover and Prisoner's Base and Run Sheep Run and Fox and Geese and we all knew what liverwurst was and Cheez Whiz and Spam and we all knew the story of Daniel in the lion's den and Noah's Ark and the Prodigal Son and a couple hundred other basic tales—I'd hate to think that little Hmong and Mexican children might go through the St. Paul public schools and not learn *O say can you see any bedbugs on me* and *On top of Old Smokey all covered with sand I shot my poor teacher with a big rubber band* and *Mine eyes have seen the glory of the burning of the school.* And of course *Step on a crack and break your mother's back.* Thanks to this wise saying, millions of youngsters have learned something about mercy and also avoided tripping on cracks and skinning their knees.

My wife and I lived in New York City for a while, a gorgeous place if you enjoy humanity, but then we begat a little girl, and we brought her home to Minnesota so she could enjoy her aunts and grow up among slow-spoken enigmatic people. (Are they—a. resolute, b. bored, c. thoughtful, d. drugged?) These are My People. I attended the University of Minnesota and remember how the marching band came blazing down University Avenue, flags snapping in the wind, the *shap-shap-shap* of their shoes, drums pounding out the cadence, and wheeled into Memorial Stadium packed with 61,000 people and when they stood and sang "firm and strong, united are we," you could feel that union in your shoes as thousands of gold balloons rose in the October air and you felt blessed to be one of this hardy northern tribe, honest and true, camped along the Mississippi River and the world's largest freshwater lake, the state that produced Fitzgerald and the Mayo Clinic and Lindbergh, and Sinclair Lewis and Hubert Humphrey. I want my daughter to be from here too. As the song says, *Like the stream that bends to sea, like the pine that seeks the blue, Minnesota still for thee, thy sons and daughters true.* When I stand at a urinal, it's the thought of Minnehaha Falls that loosens up my plumbing, and when I need to sleep at night, it's the 87 counties of Minnesota that I slowly recite and I drop off around Pennington, Pipestone, Polk, Pope, *Ramsey.* Which is where St. Paul is, a civil place in which to bring up a child. A city of yellow-dog Democrats—*not even one (1) precinct in St. Paul voted for our current Republican U.S. senator even though in his days as a Democrat he was mayor of St. Paul, that's how Democratic we are*—so there is a high value placed on public services. If you call 911 in St. Paul, the cops or the EMTs

will arrive within four minutes. In the Republican suburbs, where No New Taxes is the beginning and end of
politics and emergency services depend on volunteers,
the response time can be anywhere between ten or fifteen and thirty minutes.

This is the difference between Democrats and Republicans in 2004, when it comes right down to it. Republicans are all about Old Glory and school prayer and the
sanctity of marriage and the Fatherhood of God but
when it comes to actually needing help from them, you
shouldn't get your hopes up. They might send an ambulance or they might just send a Get Well card. In yellow-
dog St. Paul, you will be rescued by the St. Paul fire
department and there is no better emergency service
anywhere in the civilized world. You may be flat on the
floor feeling as if an elephant stepped on your chest, or
your child may have swallowed a fistful of God knows
what medication, or your grandma may have slipped on
the ice and banged her noggin and she insists she's okay
but in Swedish—whatever your dilemma, the St. Paul
rescue squad will deal with it in swift and professional
fashion. Because we Democrats feel that the people of St.
Paul are entitled to the best when it comes to what's cru-

cial. You can be a Christian, atheist, Buddhist, nudist, and the rescue squad will be there for you within four minutes.

Republicans have perfectly nice manners, normal hair, pleasant smiles, good deodorants, but when it comes down to cases, you do not want them to be monitoring your oxygen flow: they will set it to the minimum required to sustain basic brain function, and then they will recite a little prayer for you. They are a party that is all about perceptions, the Christian party that conceals enormous glittering malice and is led by brilliant bandits who are dividing and conquering the sweet land I grew up in. I don't accept this.

We Democrats are deciduous. We fade, lose heart, become torpid, languish, then the sap rises again, and we are passionate. This is a year for passion.

Chapter 2

WE HAVE BECOME THE
TEDIOUS CONSERVATIVES

There once was a good Democrat
Who was able to talk through his hat.
Such smart things he said
Off the top of his head
Or else out the place where he sat.

SOMETHING has gone seriously haywire with the Republican Party. Once, it was the party of pragmatic Main Street businessmen in steel-rimmed spectacles who decried profligacy and waste, were devoted to their communities, and supported the sort of prosperity that raises all ships. They were good-hearted people who had vanquished the gnarlier elements of their party, the paranoid Roosevelt-haters, the Flat Earthers and Prohibitionists, the antipapist antiforeigner element. The genial Eisenhower was their man, a genuine American hero of D-Day, who made it okay for reasonable people to vote Republican (even in the South), and he brought the Korean War to a stalemate, produced the Interstate Highway System, declined to rescue the French colonial army in Vietnam, and gave us a period of peace and prosperity, in which (oddly) American arts and letters flourished mightily and higher education burgeoned and there was a degree of plain *decency* in the country. Much too much was made of Alger Hiss and the Hollywood Ten by lefties with a bad case of the yips. Fifties Republicans were giants compared to today's. Richard Nixon was the last Republican leader to feel a Christian obligation toward the poor.

In the years between Nixon and Newt Gingrich, the party migrated southward down the Twisting Trail of Rhetoric and sneered at the idea of public service and became the Scourge of Liberalism, the Great Crusade Against the Sixties, the Death Star of Government, a gang of pirates famed for bold symbolic forays that diverted and fascinated the media by their sheer chutzpah, such as the misty-eyed flag-waving of Ronald Reagan who, while George McGovern flew bombers in World

War II, took a pass and made training films in Long Beach. The Willie Horton ads of 1988. The flogging of the undeserving poor, the barely concealed racism, the drumbeat of diatribes against The Gummint. The Nixon moderate vanished like the passenger pigeon, purged by a legion of angry white men who had risen to power on pure punk politics, nasty, violent, borderline psychopath. "Bipartisanship is another term for date rape," says Grover Norquist, the Sid Vicious of the GOP. "I don't want to abolish government. I simply want to reduce it to the size where I can drag it into the bathroom and drown it in the bathtub." The boy has Oedipal problems and government is his daddy.

The party of Lincoln and Liberty was transmogrified into the party of hairy-backed swamp developers and corporate shills, faith-based economists, see-through fundamentalist bullies with Bibles, Christians of convenience, freelance racists, hobby cops, misanthropic frat boys, lizardskin cigar monkeys, jerktown romeos, ninja dittoheads, the shrieking midgets of AM radio, tax cheats, cheese merchants, cat stranglers, taxi dancers, grab-ass executives, gun fetishists, genteel pornographers, pill pushers, chronic nappers, nihilists in golf

pants, backed-up Baptists, Crips and Bloods of the board-
room, panjandrums of Ponzi marketing and the grand
pooh-bahs of Percodan, censors, spin dentists, Swiss
bankers, hit men, body snatchers, mouth breathers and
tongue thrusters, testosterone junkies, oversexed hedge-
hogs, brownshirts in pinstripes, sweatshop tycoons, line
jumpers, randy preachers, marsupial moms and chirpy
news anchors, UFO scholars, johns, shroomheads, hacks,
fakirs, aggressive dorks, wizened aliens, aluminum-sid-
ing salesmen, Lamborghini libertarians, people who believe Neil Armstrong's moonwalk was filmed in Roswell,
New Mexico, little honkers out to diminish the rest of
us, braying, smirking, scratching on the national blackboard, Newt's evil spawn and their Etch-a-Sketch president with a voice like a dial tone, who for almost four
years has looked as if he were just about to say something smart, not much introspection going on here, no
inquiring minds eager to learn about the world, not
much chance of anyone picking up a book that isn't on
the official reading list and hearing a still small voice, a
dull and rigid man suspicious of the free flow of infor-
mation and of secular institutions in general, whose phi-
losophy is a jumble of badly sutured body parts trying to

walk, supported by millions of good folks who do not share the anarchist dream but sleep well with this West Texas sphinx for a nightlight. Republicans: the No. 1 reason why the rest of the world thinks we're deaf, dumb, and dangerous.

What gorgeous characters they have given us, a cast worthy of Dickens — the oily and toxic DeLay, the lubricious Lott, the bland and arrogant Dr. Frist, the shabby and devious Rove, the meathead Hastert, the squinty Rumsfeld, the stone-brained Cheney, and the tragic Powell, the Company Man Who Could Have Been Great, who was offered the mantle by all the polls but deferred to the Boss's Callow Son and vouched for him, the battlefield veteran defending the goldbricker, the bootstrap hero kneeling to the Young Pretender. Rich ironies abound! Lies pop up like toadstools in the forest! Wild swine crowd round the public trough! Outrageous gerrymandering! Districts shaped like orthopedic devices! Pocket lining on a massive scale! Paid lobbyists sit in the committee rooms and write legislation to alleviate the suffering of billionaires! Young Republicans ride the government gravy train! The train is full! More cars are added! Hypocrisies shine like cat turds in the moonlight! O Mark Twain, where art thou at this hour? Arise, and behold the Gilded Age reincarnated gaudier than ever, upholding great wealth as the sure sign of Divine Grace, railing against the expense of public schools and calling for more prisons. Henry Mencken, you poisoned these boobs and they've come back hardier than ever. A whole new strain, more virulent than any previous.

Every satirist who drew breath has flung pots of ink at this parade of tooting lummoxes and here it is come round again, marching down Main Street, rallying to the cause of William McKinley, hail, hail, the gang's all here, ta-ra-ra-BOOM-de-ay.

*

It's the natural cycle of life, I suppose, that conservatives become anarchists and liberals conservatives. Once we Democrats were young and rebellious and lobbed eggs at the bewigged and berobed Establishment and now we're the parents with the thankless job of home maintenance, defending principles that go back to the founding of the Republic, namely, the notion of the common good, the principle of equality, the very idea of representative government. We've become the tiresome, repetitive old dad who tells his boys that Progress Depends on

Teamwork and All of Us Learning to Pull Together, while the Republicans have turned into the Screw You Party. They tore into the progressive income tax, raked the IRS over the coals for chasing down deadbeats, and succeeded in convincing the American people that they are over-taxed (compared to whom? Albania?), succeeded to the extent that 17% of Americans now believe it is justifiable to cheat on your income tax.

Here in 2004, George W. Bush is running for reelection on a platform of tragedy—the single greatest failure of national defense in our history, the attacks of 9/11/2001 in which nineteen men with box cutters put this nation into a tailspin, a failure the details of which the White House has fought to keep secret, even as it has run the country into hock up to the hubcaps, thanks to generous tax cuts for the well-fixed, hoping to lead us into a box canyon of debt that will render government impotent, even as we engage in a war against a small country that was undertaken for the President's personal satisfaction but sold to the American public on the basis of brazen misinformation, a war whose purpose is to distract us from an enormous transfer of wealth taking place in this country, flowing upward, and the deception is working beautifully so far. The top 1% holds nearly half of the financial wealth, the greatest concentration of wealth of any industrialized nation, more concentrated than at any time since the Depression. In 1980, on average, CEOs earned 42 times the salary of the average worker, and these days they earn about 476 times that salary. Since 1980, the rich have been getting richer fast and furiously and hard-working people in the middle are sliding down the greasy slope who never imagined this could happen to them. The concentration of wealth and power in the hands of a few is the death knell of democracy. No republic in the history of humankind has survived this. The election of 2004 will say something about what happens to ours. The omens are not good.

I am a liberal and liberalism is the politics of kindness. Liberals stand for tolerance, magnanimity, community spirit, the defense of the weak against the powerful, love of learning, freedom of belief, art and poetry, city life, the very things that make America worth dying for. The people who call themselves conservatives stand for tax cuts, and further tax cuts, annual tax cuts, the only policy they know. Cut taxes. Use the refund to buy a gun and an attack dog to take with you when you drive your all-terrain vehicle through the barricades of Republicanville to make a foray into enemy territory to purchase supplies. They are leading this great land toward a Lost New World where Social Security and Medicare will be dim memories and America will be a series of malls connected by interstates, and people will live in walled compounds with moats, like in the Middle Ages.

Other liberals, bless their hearts, are deeply into diversity and thanks to them the public school dasn't use the word *Christmas* without mentioning *Kwanzaa*, *Hanukkah*, and *Ramadan* in the same sentence, but I am far more interested in middleness and centrality and ordinary decency, which we are losing in George W. Bush's America. He is leading our beloved country down the old plank road toward Plantation Days in Dixie, where you are either landed aristocracy, or a supervisor, or a barefoot field hand in overalls. This is not the America I grew up in.

What liberals must conserve is the middle class: the stable family who can afford to enjoy music and theater and take the kids to Europe someday and put money in the collection plate and save for college and keep up the home and be secure against catastrophe. This family has taken big hits in payroll taxes and loss of buying power and a certain suppressed panic about job security. Its optimism and good humor are not boundless and if Democrats don't defend it, it could be washed away along with the old-fashioned notion of the common good that was strong back in my youth in the Fifties when we thought of this as one nation. We learned it in public school from the Declaration of Independence and the Gettysburg Address. America is predicated on an idea, which is equality, and the equal right to life, liberty, and the pursuit of happiness. We are not a herd of woolly mammoths united only for self-preservation, nor a gang of mercenaries, nor the United Federation of Caucasians or the Church of the Sacred Banner, we are a noble political experiment and when Lincoln rose on that November afternoon in 1863, after a man with three names had blown hard for two hours, he summed up in two minutes the great cause: what could be the Lord's purpose in allowing the green fields of Pennsylvania to be soaked with blood and gore if not to consecrate these United States to the ideal of government of and by and for the people?

Nothing in literature moved me so much in my

youth as the Civil War, the popular Bruce Catton histories, the letters of soldiers, the Brady photographs, Whitman's *Specimen Days,* the biographies of Lincoln, the story of our own First Minnesota that charged forward to plug a hole at Gettysburg and save the Union line from folding—the whole epic sweep of the War and the cavalier arrogance of the South that pushed the nation to conflict and that almost put to rout the muddling patriots of the North, the stubbornness of Grant, the cult of Lee, the woozy romantic twaddle of the Lost Cause, and the mystical sense of Union that rose from the slaughter. Union: a house divided cannot stand. Slavery was a gross insult to the national ideal; we could not tolerate it and still be the United States.

If the powerful have free rein to stomp on the weak, then the Union itself is weakened: to tolerate injustice will corrupt politics and leach away public happiness and darken public places; walking in the darkened streets we will regard each other with suspicion and feel the need for locked gates, private security guards, moats, towers, motion detectors, prisons in which to keep the vengeful, and circuses and spectacles to distract us from what is happening.

The Union does not rest on strength of arms or financial wealth but on the common faith of American people that their children have a fair chance to thrive, that the iron gates have not slammed shut on them, that there is justice, that the Bill of Rights has not been privatized. This is the bottom line in America: we have to feel that our kids stand a chance—otherwise, there's a civil war brewing.

We are one country, and I remain a proud Unionist, happy to sing "The Star-Spangled Banner" and pledge allegiance, sing about the amber waves of grain, wish I was in the land of cotton, pick my teeth with a carpet tack, be in the kitchen with Dinah, hate to see the evening sun go down, take myself out to the ball game, walk that lonesome valley, and lean on the everlasting arms. I love this country. This is one of those simple dumb discoveries a man makes, like the night I came out of the New York hospital where I, a bystander at my wife's travail, had held my naked newborn six-pound shining-eyed daughter in my two hands, and I walked around town at midnight stunned by the fact that what I had seen was utterly ordinary, *everybody comes into the world pretty much like that.* In the same spirit, I walk around St. Paul and think, *This is a great country* and it wasn't made so by angry people. We have a sacred duty to bequeath it to our grandchildren in better shape than however we found it. We have a long way to go and we're not getting any younger.

The Union is what needs defending this year. Government of Enron and by Halliburton and for the southern Baptists is not the same as what Lincoln spoke of. Not even close. This gang of Pithecanthropus Republicanii has humbugged us to death on terrorism and tax cuts for the comfy and school prayer and flag burning and claimed the right to know what books we read and to dump their sewage upstream from town and clear-cut the forest and gut the IRS and promote the corporate takeover of the public airwaves and to hell with anybody who opposes them. Their crusade against government has given patriotism a bad name. And their victory has been accompanied by such hubris as would choke a goat. One Republican columnist wrote that Democrats should give up opposing tax breaks for the rich because working people don't vote their self-interest, they vote their aspirations and are happy to give big gifts to rich people because they hope to become rich too. A little TV Republican named Tucker Carlson wrote a column saying that if Democrats want to win, they need to (1) talk tough, (2) start their own think tanks, and (3) get a sense of humor.—(3) Got one, Tucker, (2) got plenty of think tanks, except we call them colleges, and (1) shut your piehole, peabrain, or I'll set fire to your loafers.

Democrats have changed America in simple basic ways in the past fifty years that have benefited everyone. Race has become less and less an issue in people's lives and racism has ceased to be socially acceptable anywhere. Women have moved into every realm of society and this is everywhere accepted without much comment. Equal opportunity in education, employment, housing. There is general agreement on the right to a dignified old age, guaranteed by the state. Democrats led the way in bringing these things about. It's one thing to get into power and do favors for your friends; it's quite another to touch the conscience of a nation. The last Republican to do that was Teddy Roosevelt.

Chapter 3

WHERE I'M COMING FROM

I WAS BORN in 1942, in time to catch glimpses of fugitive scenes from the 19th Century and get coal smoke in my nostrils and hear the *oomph* of steam engines in the night and the scream of their whistles. Somber women in plain print dresses walked through my childhood quoting proverbs (Haste makes waste. If wishes were horses, then beggars would ride and the world be drowned in a sea of pride) and men whose faces looked carved from wood and who kept a heavy-lidded watch on things. I rode the hayrack drawn by Belgian horses, harness jingling, tossing their heads, and once I rode one bareback, clinging to his mane, utter gooseflesh grandeur at the age of four. I stood next to Uncle Jim, his forehead against the flank of a cow, and smelled the warm milk squirting into the steel bucket and poured it into a milk can to be lowered into a cistern in the milk house and kept cool until the milk truck came to pick it up. I chased chickens through the lilac bushes and grabbed their ankles with a coat hanger and brought them to the chopping block to be dispatched. On Sunday mornings, I sat on hard wooden chairs next to stern old white-bearded Plymouth Brethren in black gabardine suits and white starched shirts buttoned to the top, no ties, no vain adornments, who walked the narrow path of truth and righteousness, intent on finding the Lord's Will for their lives; they put Him first and material things second, as a result of which they were poor and lived on the fringe of society, which was more or less what Jesus had promised His followers, so they were not disappointed. They were not much for small talk and they didn't trust strangers or confide in them. On their best days they were funny and generous and sociable, and on their worst days, they didn't discuss it. They were stubborn stoics who got up at dawn and washed their faces in cold water from steel basins and read a chapter of Scripture and prayed at length and then worked until dusk and had supper and fell into bed early. They bought no insurance and had no faith in doctors. They accepted disease as their lot in life and pain to be cheerfully endured and walked down the narrow road that life assigned them, walked to the end knowing it was not the end but only a corner around which Christ awaited them in shining glory, His loving arms open to receive them. They were people of profound kindness.

I am descended from an act of kindness. My grandfather James Keillor journeyed from New Brunswick to Minnesota in 1880 to help out his brother-in-law who had homesteaded north of Anoka and was dying of tuberculosis. (James's grandfather Thomas Keillor came over to Canada from Yorkshire in 1773 and tried to make a living harvesting hay in the saltwater meadows that French settlers had been driven from, and here the Keillors met up with the Crandalls, who had fled north from the Connecticut colonies in 1778, having taken a stand for law and order at the wrong moment in history and lost their homes, everything they couldn't haul away in a wagon. Premature conservatives.) James was 20, a strapping young shipwright, and he arrived in Anoka to find the brother-in-law on his deathbed, the sister with three small children and a modest farm on sandy soil along

Trott Brook in Ramsey Township. James stayed to raise those children, and then, at the age of 46, fell in love with a 20-year-old teacher, Dora Powell, whose schoolhouse was across the road from the farm. One day, he crossed the road and told her he wanted to kiss her, and he did, or she did, or something happened between them, and they were married by a justice, and he brought her home. In his hurry to get upstairs he forgot his team of horses, and they stood there all night in harness. From this passionate union sprang several hundred Keillors including me.

I was born in Anoka, Minnesota, early enough to see horse-drawn plowing and experience the darkness of a nonelectrified farm and late enough to be only thirteen when Elvis blew into town and was fervently condemned by all serious right-thinking people and Jerry Lee Lewis shook our nerves and rattled our brains. I got to hear a roomful of Brethren sing a cappella the mournful old hymns and baptize young people in Trott Brook and I saw the last living veteran of the Union Army, Albert Woolson, ride in the Anoka Halloween parade, an ancient cadaverous man sunk deep in the backseat of a convertible and waving a flag in his tiny translucent hand, and I got to hear Jack Benny on the radio, but I was still young enough to be 18 when John F. Kennedy ran for President and to be bowled over by him.

Grandma lived on the farm with Uncle Jim and they didn't read the paper or listen to the radio much. Uncle Jim had a crystal set in his room but I don't recall them ever discussing politics. Presidents came and went, and the great and famous, on a stage very far away from their thoughts. (In 1961, the year before Grandma died, I made her sit down and watch John Glenn's rocket blast into orbit, but nothing could make her believe it was true. Pictures held no truth for her, and Walter Cronkite was nobody she believed whatsoever; after all, she'd never met him.)

My dad had left the farm when he was 23 and eloped with my mother and went to work in the post office. After the war, he bought an acre of cornfield north of Minneapolis and started building us a house with money borrowed under the GI Bill of Rights. We were living in Minneapolis where big yellow streetcars with cane seats rumbled down Bloomington Avenue past our house and we rode the trolley to Como Zoo and the great glass-domed Conservatory and the old green wooden ballpark to see the Millers and to Grandpa Denham's little stucco bungalow on Oakland Avenue under the elms overarching the green yards, the peonies and marigolds, the cast-iron lawn chairs, the bird bath, the gazing globe, the trim grass, a world of perfect order, the streets numbered and the avenues alphabetical from Aldrich, Bryant, Colfax, Dupont through Washburn, Xerxes, York, and Zenith. In my memory, my movie-star-handsome dad stands in his wool overcoat, a gray fedora on his head, smiling at the Revere movie camera in Mother's hand as a streetcar passes in the summer of 1947. He smiles, like Gary Cooper. We children stand perfectly still in Grandpa's yard and then we perk up and smile—someone off-camera has told us to—and like good children we do and my sister waves.

Dad dug the basement for the new house in the clay and loam, poured concrete, lay concrete block walls, put a roof over it, and we left Minneapolis and lived in the basement for five years while he framed up the house and finished it, a three-bedroom Cape Cod, white, blue shutters, from a blueprint he'd seen in *Popular Home*. The whine of the power saw, the smell of sawdust, the rhythm of the hammer. He worked for the Railway Mail

Service, sorting mail in the mail car between St. Paul and Jamestown, N.D., going off to work in the afternoon, in overalls, with a government-issue .38 revolver in a holster, and put in a 12-hour shift, slept at the Cran Hotel in Jamestown, then boarded the eastbound for another shift.

To our Keillor cousins, we were city people and looked upon with some suspicion so we tried to win their approval and pitch in with chores, shovel cow manure, do our part, not flinch. My mother, a city girl, learned to dip a dead chicken in boiling water, rip off its feathers, take a butcher knife and gut it, without comment.

The big hurdle for me was the outhouse, sitting there and dropping your dirt into a hole and hearing it plop on other people's and at night, if your bladder was full, feeling your way to the end of the bed and locating the chamber pot and squatting on it and doing your business. Our house that Dad built had indoor plumbing of course and this permitted great delicacy in regard to personal matters. You locked the door, ran water in the sink to camouflage other sounds, and nobody was any the wiser. It was a shock to go to the farm and sit in the old two-holer and be joined by your cousin. At first you tried to pretend nothing was happening, that you'd only come here to peruse the Sears catalog and its fine selection of sporting goods, but then events took their course, your bowels opened, a great stink was launched downward, and you were initiated into the great democracy of the latrine: *WE ALL DO IT.*

Living in the basement, climbing the stairs to the muddy cornfield, piles of sand and gravel, I got my first inkling that *we were poor.* Startling to a boy of six. Other people live in houses with carpets and antimacassars and dresser scarves and figurines and we live in a bunker in the ground. *Bunker, bunkbed.* How poor are we? *I don't know.* We had a half-acre vegetable garden and in late summer Mother canned. In the laundry room stood a wall of shelves with rows of Ball fruit jars, filled with corn, beans, and stewed tomatoes. In early spring, Dad and I drove north to Lake Superior for smelting late at night: a bonfire on the shore near the mouth of the Lester River, a crowd of men in hip waders, and when there was a run of smelt rushing for the river to spawn, the crowd waded in with landing nets and hauled up pound after pound of the little fish and we took ours home in big milk cans and filleted and froze them, to be eaten over the summer, breaded and fried. This seemed to me to be poor people food because it was free.

One day, helping Dad bring groceries into the basement from the car, I carried two big three-gallon glass jugs of milk, one in each hand, as I'd seen Uncle Jim carry milk cans from the barn. Toted them down the back stairs and then lost my balance, pitched forward, dropped the jugs, which broke. Six gallons of milk sploshed on the concrete floor. I picked up the shards of glass, deeply ashamed, and slunk into the room I shared with my brother and lay on my bunk and sobbed into the pillow. I had wasted food. We were poor. What would happen to us now? The pillowcase was wet with my tears. Our old black cocker spaniel, Capadocia, lay at my feet. *We are poor.* On the other hand, I had books, a tablet and pencils, a radio, a pair of binoculars. Clean clothes.

When the garage got built, I liked to put a little piece of plywood on the floor and stand, bat in hand, and wait on the 3-and-2 pitch and swing, driving Whitey Ford's fastball over the centerfield fence in Yankee Stadium to win the seventh game of the World Series for the New York Giants. I earned $100,000 a year and had bought a fine home for my family, a real showplace with chandeliers, and all my aunts and uncles were proud as punch, and I had a wife, a beautiful one but vague, faraway in the stands, cheering, waving a hanky.

I sometimes tried to help Dad with building the house, but he wasn't a great teacher. He got disgusted if you made the same mistake twice. So I holed up in my room and read books, Richard Halliburton's sailing expeditions to the Far East, *Five Little Peppers and How They Grew, Black Beauty, Heidi*. And then jumped to *Main Street* and *Babbitt* and Fitzgerald and *Studs Lonigan*. Writing was respected in our family. Not necessarily fiction, but literary endeavor was honored by my mother and father, who revered the King James Bible of course and enjoyed a clever turn of phrase in the newspaper. Mother followed Cedric Adams's tales of his boyhood in Madelia in the *Star*. Writing was something of a black art, and there were bad characters in that line of work, drunkards, infidels, adulterers, but the power of language was respected. I was honored when my father asked me when I was 19 to write a letter for him, setting out his qualifications to be a rural mail carrier, and I did a good workmanlike job on it, though he didn't get the position.

Qualifications didn't matter so much; it was a patronage appointment, and Dad didn't know the right people.

My father sat at one end of the table, my mother at the other, six children, three on a side, and we passed the stewed tomatoes, the green beans, the liver and onions, and I kept wondering, *Are we poor?* We went up to the farm in Anoka to kill chickens, which seemed like a poor-person thing to do. The chickens ran like halfbacks through the lilac bushes and into the cornfield, but I ran most of them down and hooked them by the ankles with a wire hanger and brought them flapping and croaking back to Dad, who dispatched them with an ax on a bloody stump. I held the carcass until it stopped dripping and gave it to Mother for defeathering and evisceration. Dad said that store-bought chicken didn't taste as good to him and Grandma said you could never be sure whether store-bought meat was properly handled. *No, it's because we're poor.* On long car trips, my mother made sandwiches on a cutting board across her lap sitting in the front seat, cheese and baloney or peanut butter and jelly. She said the prices you pay for food in restaurants are outlandish. *Poor people.* Up on the farm, I washed my face with Lava soap in cold water in the morning and wiped it on a towel on a roller. I collected eggs and brought them in for breakfast, fried in a black crusted skillet on a woodstove, with a thick slice of Grandma's bread. Once I swung on a rope through the dusty air of the haymow and leaped onto a stack of bales and skidded down the side of them through the open hatch and into the bull's pen and cracked my head on his feed trough and was carried into the house and laid on the couch and Grandma put brown paper on my head. I thought I should go to the hospital but she moistened this brown paper and placed it on the contusions and said it'd make me feel better. *We are poor people,* I thought. *We cannot afford to go to a doctor. Other people would take their children to be x-rayed after a bump on the head but in our family we put paper on them and say a prayer, Help Us Again Amen, and that's the end of it.*

I think of my mother at the sink peeling potatoes and looking out at the snowy garden and the wash frozen stiff on the clotheslines, and she is angry at my dad who has criticized what she spent for Christmas presents. She defers to him, though she works as hard as he, maybe harder. She does the laundry in a washing machine with a wringer and hangs it on the line and scrubs the floors and cooks and vacuums and in late summer she takes all the bounty of the garden and cooks it in a pressure cooker to be canned in jars. You make a mistake in the canning process and you run the risk of *Clostridium botulinum*, which is so deadly that an ounce could kill 100 million people. One jar of asparagus, the equivalent of a medium-range nuclear warhead. (You tap the lid with a knife and if it rings, then the seal is good and the angel of death will pass over, and if it thuds, you throw that jar away.) She puts up a hundred jars of tomatoes and a hundred quarts of corn and makes pickles and jam, all for frugality's sake, and she doesn't remind him of the money he spends to buy a new car every few years. She can't mention this for fear he will turn silent, which is his weapon. Hers is weeping, and lamentation, his is walking away and getting busy with something. She was one of those women who never read fashion magazines, never updated their look, never used hairspray, just put on a scarf. One of those women who got up every morning and got the kids off to school and did the wash and every spring went at the house in a fury of soap and Lysol and scrubbed and scraped and rendered everything shining and new and yet had not much say in things in general, having been brought up to be of service and accept a rough road without complaining, women of great kindness.

My grandma had no luxuries and no expectation of any, but her children felt the gravitational pull of prosperity. They left the farm and got jobs in town and wore town clothes and street shoes and didn't necessarily read Scripture after breakfast or kneel and pray, just a quick rote prayer over the food, because they had to be to work on time. They lived cheek-to-jowl with strangers and learned to make small talk and bought chicken at Super Valu and got a TV set and started believing Walter Cronkite. But still they thought about God all the time. A plaque hung on our dining room wall (CHRIST THE UNSEEN GUEST AT EVERY MEAL, THE SILENT LISTENER TO EVERY CONVERSATION) to remind us that we were on His Mind and after dinner we circulated the little plastic bread loaf with the Scripture verse cards and each person at the table drew a card and read a verse. *We know that all things work together for good to those who love God.* Chuck Berry was cruising along in his Coupe de Ville and Elvis bumping and grinding and the Beach Boys sang anthems to California, but the basic question in my mind, then and now, is *What does God want me to do?* I think about this every day. Or I try not to think about it and thus think even harder about it. *Love the Lord thy God with all thy heart and all thy might. And love thy neighbor as thyself.* I sit and ponder this with the trash culture bumping and grinding outside the window and the powerful undertow of narcissism tugging, and I believe I serve God and my neighbor by paying diligent, prayerful, and playful attention to my peculiar gifts, such as they are, and doing good work that supports the weak and lightens up the heavy. I belong to the Church of Work and Prayer. I was young in the time of hippiedom and flittery-skittery tie-dye people in flowing locks with their dreamy take on things and long yawps about illusion/reality and druggy sitar-ridden music and they were not from my church. I knew an English major drop-out who felt a holy calling to raise sheep and live like a medieval serf in a makeshift yurt while making helpless animals miserable whom he had no idea how to herd or care for. Not my church. Coke and speed and marijuana didn't interest me for some reason and we Christians have no need of barbiturates, we are sleepy enough as it is.

My politics doesn't come from the Sixties, it comes from my parents' generation who stepped out of high school into the Depression, hoed corn, drove truck, pumped gas, made do, bopped around on not much dough, went off in 1942 and fought the good war and came home and enjoyed the democratic prosperity of the Fifties. Satirists portrayed them as anti-intellectuals and raging conformists in love with plastic and the color beige, but I think they were just happy they had come through so much trouble and danger and had a roof over their heads and food on the table. They were public-spirited, joiners of committees, school board stalwarts, volunteer firemen, softball coaches, Scoutmasters, Sunday School teachers, and the women—this was back before it took two people working 60-hour weeks to support a middle-class family—were ferocious do-gooders in the community, the angels of the library, the muscle behind the school bond issue, the church ladies, the sur-rogate mothers, organizers of festivals, tireless fund-raisers. Sometimes satirists are dead wrong. What seemed like conformity was really a low level of narcissism and no taste for flamboyant behavior: my parents and their contemporaries believed in a sort of public happiness that found full expression at Anoka High School graduation—the wave of warm buttery emotion at the playing of "Pomp and Circumstance" and the singing of the national anthem, the flashbulbs popping as the children processed in, the good feelings for teachers and school and community, even if the speaker was a dud and a windbag. The loyalty to the community was palpable.

My politics is somehow descended from the kindness of my aunts, apolitical though they were, from tireless Aunt Elsie who kept a lovely home, so clean and fragrant, her perfect Sunday dinners, her exquisite hospitality, and Aunt Ina with her collection of seven hundred sets of salt and pepper shakers, and Aunt Ruth, short and round with sweet little chins and fat creases at her wrists, like a baby's, her plump feet in high heel pumps, the first photographer in the family, and Aunt Josephine with her well-kept garden, the handsomest woman in the family, and Aunt Bessie, the family historian and wit, and Aunt Eleanor who marshaled the big Keillor family Thanksgivings for years, an outdoorswoman who skied and kept horses and cut trees and drove around to check on her elderly neighbors almost up to the day she died, in her kitchen, fixing Thanksgiving dinner. I do not remember these Christian women as judgmental or sarcastic or authoritarian: they were the soul of kindness and their spirit points to the politics that sees to children, the sick, the poor, the wayward, the downcast, and lets the slick and the strong do for themselves.

Yes, my ancestors made a bigger impression on me than any of my contemporaries did, especially the addled ones. I'm conservative. I went to the contemporary service at church where the young minister played guitar and the kids sang, "Wherever I am, you're near me, nobody cares for me as you do, you give me all that I need. Thank you, Lord, for helping me as you do." And I really do prefer *Rock of Ages cleft for me, let me hide myself in thee.* It's better writing, no matter what anybody says. My ancestors told me, in plain Protestant fashion, to Work, Achieve, Be Somebody, Question Authority, Don't Be a Chip on the Tide, Be Your Own Man. The glib Sixties talk about the system being broken struck me as juvenile and silly: if water flows from the tap and the buses run and the mailman brings the mail and the newspaper lands on your porch in the morning with a fiery editorial against ignorance and corruption, the system is working okay—the rest is up to you. I could appreciate the Christian aspects of hippiedom, the communalism, the embrace of poverty, the love of the land, the tolerance, the cheery potluck suppers and the singing and barefoot dancing, the open-heartedness, but the writing—oh my God. A thin soup of mystical noodles and no salt, pages and pages of transcendent dishwater and nobody home.

My generation went from the pretentious Bob Dylan to arguing about wine and cheese and the virginity of their olive oil and the merits of vintage balsamic vinegars, coffee beans and designer jeans and shiatsu vs. reflexologic massage. They lived most intensely through media, were happy jargonizers, and sadly self-absorbed— they could talk for hours about a romance gone sour and pick at an ancient grudge against their father and ponder their fate until you were desperate for an excuse to leave. No, my politics comes from my parents, who believed in keeping your yard nice and paying your taxes and looking out for people in trouble. The descendants of the narcissist New Agers are the narcissist Republicans.

People with too much money and too little character, all sensibility and no sense, all nostalgia and no history. It's the Republican Party that followed its nose and swung to the right and I am standing where my people stood back when this was one country, before the deluge of delusion.

Chapter 4

⚭ ○ ○ ○ ○ ○ ○ ○ ○ ○ ⚯ ○ ○ ○ ○ ○ ○ ○ ○ ⚭

ANOKA HIGH SCHOOL

I AM A CHILD of public education. My parents had six children and there was no choice but to put their trust in the Anoka public schools. They packed me off to Benson School on the day after Labor Day, 1948, with lunch money in a small brown envelope and a tablet and pencils in a pencil box and told me to keep my nose clean and do what the teacher said. Mrs. Shaver was my first grade teacher, St. Estelle, who noticed I was slow to read and kept me after school to read aloud to her as she corrected papers and made me feel I was doing this to keep her entertained, not because I was dumb. Though I was. At movies, when the text rolled down at the beginning,

"Many years ago in Europe during the era known as the Dark Ages, bands of knights roamed the countryside . . ." I was lost and other kids were not.

Parents did not supervise their children's schooling then, just as they didn't manage our social lives— "parenting" wasn't a verb and children didn't have "play dates," we just went out the door and fell into some company or other, a band of robbers, or the Confederate cavalry, or an Ojibway war party, and as for school, Mother looked at the class projects I brought home and commented on the penmanship, and she looked at the report card when Mrs. Shaver sent it home, but teachers were deferred to back then. And so, amazingly, we learned "Frankie and Johnny" in the fourth grade, a traditional ballad about a pimp and a prostitute—unthinkable now—including the lines:

> *The first time she shot him he staggered.*
> *The second time she shot him he fell.*
> *The third time there was a southwest wind*
> *From the northeast corner of hell.*

There we are in the class photograph, Benson School, 1952: the girls in corduroy jumpers and the boys in plaid shirts, our hair slicked down and combed, our clean hands folded on the desks, the map of the United States of America in the back of the room. We aren't handsome or stylish children, as children today are, and we didn't bathe every day, just on Saturday night, and in between we washed our faces, no deodorant for us, we smelled like kids, but we were extremely anxious to please and most of us, thanks to Mrs. Shaver and Mrs. Moehlenbrock, loved school. I'm in the second row from the left, fifth desk from the front, the boy in steel-rim glasses, the good speller, competing with Billy Pedersen for Champion Reader honors. My mother made sure I had clean clothes, some from the Sears, Roebuck catalog and some handed down from older cousins and one pair of jeans from my sister that zipped up the side. Mother reminded me to say, "Please" and "Excuse me" and "May I—" (not "Can I—") and to pay attention in school and not daydream. A report card with poor marks in deportment was not taken lightly. Grandma Keillor had been a schoolteacher and her grandchildren were not going to be scofflaws and scapegraces and illiterate ne'er-do-wells. A mark of Satisfactory in arithmetic demanded a promise to reform and earn an Excellent. It wasn't enough to say you weren't interested in arithmetic. Maybe you weren't but you should pay attention and learn something and not waste the teacher's time.

For 7th grade, I got on the yellow schoolbus and rode it ten miles north to Anoka where I spent six years in Anoka High School, where my dad had graduated and all my Keillor aunts and uncles. Anoka was a river town, on the Rum and Mississippi, with a bustling Main Street and a handsome old red-brick county courthouse with a steeple sitting high and proud in the courthouse square. A quiet town where the front-page news in the Anoka *Herald* tended toward community events and nothing bad was said about anybody.

In Anoka High School you found yourself among farm kids smelling of hay, the haberdasher's kid in his yellow cardigan sweater, and greasers in black slacks and pink shirts and hair like Elvis's, their customized cars blasting into the parking lot in the morning, and the debate team crowd who were earnest and ambitious, and the brainy kids (innocent, socially inept) and the fraternity of jocks who had to be careful not to appear brainy. Then there were the oddballs like me, outsiders, starved for approval, doinking around writing poems or drawing

cartoons or doing Bob & Ray comedy routines or thinking about space travel. We were celibates, unkissed by
anybody, our dignity was too brittle to risk rejection. I
read self-help books, such as we had in 1958, and they
said, "Just be yourself," which, in my case, did not seem
to me a good idea.

I wasn't very bright but I disguised my ordinariness
by being extremely quiet so some teachers imagined I
was an introspective genius. Others wondered if I were
deaf. A person almost always burnishes his reputation
by shutting up: I learned that as a boy. I practiced the art
of invisibility, the gift of the middle child in a large family, a sort of vacancy or blankness, and teachers looked
right through me and asked the person behind me to
come to the blackboard and work out the math problem,
and girls looked through me as if I were foliage. I didn't
mind.

I was six-foot-three, 136 pounds with my shoes on, I
looked like a folded ironing board with hair, I didn't go
around mirrors. I was so near-sighted that without my
glasses I lived in an impressionist world. I was in the
Young Democrats Club and the girls I knew were Democrats and sympathetic to needy cases. The club took a

ski trip to Theodore Wirth Park, my first time on skis. These were the wooden kind with the single leather strap across your shoes. I got in the back of the line at the top of the hill. I didn't use poles because I had no idea what to do with them. I pushed off from the top of the hill when nobody was looking and suddenly I was a physics experiment, trying to stay vertical, hands over my head, trees racing by, the law of gravity all over me, and a small spruce zoomed toward me, three feet high, and I leaned to one side and the ground came up and whacked me and I slid on my face for a hundred feet or so and collected a few pounds of snow under my shirt and pants, and hiked down the hill and never tried skiing again. I still remember every moment of that run. People ski for years trying to attain an intensity of experience that I got the first time. I went to the ski lodge and there was my crowd, the doinks, the gimps, the losers, hanging around the lobby fireplace and pretending to have a very very good time waiting to go home. I took a cup of spiced tea and sat down on the couch and glimpsed myself in an old cracked mirror across the room, a small dark cloud with a lizard face, inept, impoverished, faintly ludicrous, a person I wouldn't have wanted to know.

There were some lovely moments with girls, lounging in swimsuits in a dark green gazebo on a long sloping lawn by the river, and talking and smoking, trying to get the hang of cigarette inhalation and be intellectual, arguing with terrible certainty that the world had taken a fatal turn and was about to end in nuclear conflagration—a dark imagination was a sure way to be taken seriously. I longed to have a girlfriend to whisper affection to in the dark, and neck with, the little ballet of tenderness, the electricity, the delicacy of touch and countertouch—I wondered if something terrible was wrong with me that I hadn't kissed a girl yet—16, 17, 18—when did normal people start doing this? I sent away for a nudist magazine with black and white photos of naked people playing volleyball, which I read secretly in the basement and one day, hearing footsteps on the stairs, stuffed it into a bookshelf full of old *Sugar Creek Gang* and *Nancy Drew* books and fled, and never found it again. Somebody took it and threw it away, but nothing was said to me about it. We were good at silence in our family.

Altogether the Class of 1960, Anoka High School, formed a picture of democracy that I will carry for the rest of my life. We went through it all together—the embarrassment, walking to the front of speech class and turning and facing them, or standing in gym shorts and fermented socks in a line of boys waiting to do a flying somersault and thinking to myself, "Someday I won't have to do this," the dull misery of indifferent teachers (coaches were the worst), a lingering sense of dread about the future, the gathering sense of inevitable failure and disgrace. All of us odd ducks lined up in our graduation gowns and paraded onto the football field that June evening with *no idea* what life would deal out to us. Not a clue.

But it was there at Anoka High School, that big, bland beige-tiled building, that Mr. Hochstetter encouraged my literary pretensions. He was a brilliant man who paced his classroom declaiming about Twain and Mencken and George Ade and how Luther's Reformation had paved the way for social criticism like Sinclair Lewis's *Main Street* while the boys in the back of the room dozed or read comics. He liked me, and said I had talent to write, and a kind word or two is all a boy needs. The heart almost bursts with pleasure. He directed me to the Minneapolis Public Library where I climbed the stairs past the Egyptian mummy in its stone coffin and entered into the stacks and there was pure heaven. I hadn't thought about college, not considering myself slick or bright enough to make a go of it, being from Podunkville, but I was at home in a library, utterly in my element, and the University of Minnesota had an enormous library, so I would give that a try.

○ ○ ○ ○ ○ ○ ○ ○ ○ ○ ☼ ○ ○ ○ ○ ○ ○ ○ ○ ○ ○

Chapter 5

1960

They taught about sex at the Academy,
Genetics, biology, anatomy—
Which I never learned
Because my head was turned
By the girl who sat just ahademy.

I N THE FALL of 1960, I was a freshman at the University of Minnesota when John F. Kennedy came to Minneapolis to give a speech in his campaign for President. I was a tall kid, 18, close-cropped, with horn-rim glasses, in blue jeans and white shirt and corduroy jacket, and I sat in the balcony of the auditorium, to Kennedy's right, high above his head, watching him and the crowd enthralled by him, his hands in his jacket pockets, rocking forward on his toes, that brilliant grin as he stood doused in applause, glowing in the light, everyone standing and cheering for that handsome man, the way he modestly ducked his head and shook hands with the dignitaries on the dais, grinned at the audience, gripped the podium, gave a little wave to the balcony, and the applause went on and on.

In the spring, we of the Young Democrats of Anoka High School had followed our senator, Hubert H. Humphrey, in his losing battle with Kennedy in the primaries, and some of the idealists felt that Hubert got robbed in West Virginia, that Kennedy had bought the nomination and the machine politicians had him in their pocket. ("Machine" was our term for people who were very very good at coaxing out the vote.) My classmate Barbara read somewhere that Kennedy's father was a rum runner during Prohibition and this incensed her. We sat in our bathing suits on the grass by the beach on the Mississippi, both of us pale, shade seekers, and she poured out her bitterness that Hubert, a *true* Democrat who fought the good fight for equal rights for Negroes had been passed over in favor of the son of a crook. It just wasn't right. I didn't understand why anyone who possessed such a fabulous body as hers should be bitter, ever. She wore a one-piece white swimsuit, the top clamped on to her breasts, the bottom she kept tugging down and adjusting. She was such an idealist that I never even held hands with her. Never considered it. She was crazy about Hubert, who was a giant in Minnesota, a shining presence at the Aquatennial parade every summer, perched on the back of a white convertible, grinning, waving, always charged up in the presence of a crowd. Everyone got a kick out of seeing Hubert. But he did not travel well. In Minnesota, he seemed lively and ebullient and on the road he sounded shrill, slightly hysterical compared to Kennedy, who was the coolest politician ever, a handsome war hero with the Irish gift of spontaneous wit. Hubert was an evangelist and Kennedy was a hero, a man who looked great just saying "good morning."

Barbara went to St. Olaf College and I got a summer job as a dishwasher at the Evangeline Hotel for Women on Loring Park in Minneapolis. I started wearing a Kennedy button on my T-shirt at work, perspiring in my white apron, lugging the trays of steaming hot plates off the conveyer. Dishwashing brings out the romantic in a man. You come out of the steam and heat of the scullery with the smell of detergent in your nose, and the beauty of the world overwhelms you, an ordinary park with grass and trees is like the gardens of Versailles, and by September, when classes started, I was writing big thoughts in my journal. *Death is the admission price we pay at the end of the most wonderful show there is. There are no free tickets. Being fully alive is the only true success; to not love is a form of destruction.* I walked onto campus for the first day of classes and up the mall to Northrup Auditorium and looked up at its great pillars and the Jeffersonian inscription on the facade above, FOUNDED IN THE FAITH THAT MEN ARE ENNOBLED BY UNDERSTANDING, DEDICATED TO THE ADVANCEMENT OF LEARNING AND THE SEARCH FOR TRUTH, DEVOTED TO THE INSTRUCTION OF YOUTH AND THE WELFARE OF THE STATE. Along the mall, a stately parade of utilitarian brick buildings with pillars pasted to their fronts, a river of humanity flowing under the canopy of majestic elms, a lot of lost freshmen lolling on the steps studying campus maps and planning their route from one class to the next, and a steady procession of Africans and Indians and Pakistanis and Koreans come to study plant agronomy and engineering, Africans blacker than midnight who spoke with British accents like John Gielgud's, black

Africans speaking beautiful French (I turned and followed them, eavesdropping, so astonishing this was to hear), bearded Sikhs in turbans, women in saris with red dots painted on their foreheads, Korean War vets in fatigues and GI sunglasses, old bearded lefties in turtlenecks clutching their *I. F. Stone Weekly* and *The Realist,* cigarette-smoking women playing the role of beat princess or troubled intellect or Audrey Hepburn heroine, cool people who wore dark glasses *even in the dark,* people who might possibly have been poets. Some obvious jocks, crewcuts, jerseys, bow-legged, but a small number compared to the crowd of anxious, bookish people en route to serious encounters with history and literature. Ambition everywhere you looked, electrical currents of it jazzing the air.

I walked over to Dinkytown to buy my books at Perrine's, down the street from Al's Breakfast Nook, near Vescio's and a rats' nest of a bookstore called Heddon's whose snowy-haired proprietor, after pondering a moment, could reach into the third orange crate from the bottom and pull out the very book you asked for, and Virg 'N' Don's Grocery, the name of which appealed to me, and a coin laundry called The Tub, and McCosh's

Bookstore with the grave bearded McCosh who liked to tack up anarchist aphorisms and pictures of Orwell and Kerouac and Paul Krassner, and the Gray's Drugstore lunch counter (a grilled cheese sandwich, chili, and a vanilla shake, please) and a fine little coffeehouse called the Ten O'Clock Scholar where a beaky kid with brushy hair played a battered guitar and sang "O Fair and Tender Ladies" and *It's dark as a dungeon and damp as the dew, Where the dangers are many and the pleasures are few.* The stage was in front, before the big double plate-glass window, and sometimes a passerby stopped on the sidewalk, peered in the window, into the dark room, and then realized he was part of a show and fled.

I walked over to Folwell Hall, home of the English Department and the divine Miss Sarah Youngblood and craggy old Huntington Brown and Samuel Monk the 18th Century man and Toni McNaron who propounded Milton and Archibald Leyasmeyer the Chaucerian and other noble and learned friends of literature, and I felt grateful that this institution had opened its doors to a dreamer like me who had no clear vocation whatsoever. I was operating on a wistful urge to sit in libraries and be a writer and that was all. I wasn't like the anxious bookish people who, I assumed, were proceeding on a well-plotted course, boys climbing the slopes toward law school, smart girls in chemistry lab who would march on to distinction developing polymers. Myself, I just hoped to be lucky.

I paid $71 for a quarter's tuition and another $10 or so for my books, a political science text, a volume of Horace and a Latin dictionary, and Strunk & White's *Elements of Style* for my composition course—and notebooks with the university seal on the cover (*Omnibus Artibus, Commune Vinculum*) and I went and took a seat in the long reading room in Walter Library. Around me, men and women bent to the hard work of scholarship, folks for whom attending college was not an assumed privilege. The vets on the GI Bill and the African and Asian exchange students and all the ones who were the first in their family to attend college, whose parents' own hopes had been deferred by the Depression and the War—these students approached the U with a great chins-up pencils-sharpened sense of purpose. They sat at the long oak library tables, heads bowed, rows and rows of them, reading, reading, reading—sons of garage mechanics on their way to medical school, daughters of dairy farmers out to become professors of Romance languages—a great American migration as inspiring as anything that took place on the Oregon Trail. These pioneers craved a life in which beauty and delight and intellectual challenge are staples; they wanted to travel, read novels, go to the theater, be *smart* about the world and not reflexively pessimistic like their parents, have farflung experiences. The craving for *experiences* was powerful. Love and adventure and interesting work—a great many of us, fearing the regimentation of corporate life, would head for the burgeoning non-profit world. Such a purposeful bunch—who looked like me, were dressed like me, had no money either—who plowed through the texts and took notes and shushed up the goofballs in their midst. Boys and girls who came to the library to sit and giggle were glared at and told to be still—this never happened in high school! These were people with a sense of vocation. It was a Thomas Hart Benton mural come to life—"The Children of the Great Plains Claiming Their Birthright." Their once-in-a-lifetime chance to realize their God-given talent, as medical technicians or scholars of medieval painting or the operas of Verdi or the breeding rituals of the Arctic ptarmigan. No guarantee of success, or even of gainful employment. Pure free enterprise.

Dad had made it clear that he couldn't contribute to pay for my education, which I hadn't asked him to and I was relieved not to have to consider an offer. A nice clean break. I got a job working the 6 to 10 A.M. shift in the big parking lot on the river flats for $1.48 an hour. Nine hundred cars, and it filled up by 7:30 so there you were with a couple hours of paid study time. You learned to ignore your fellow parking lot attendant who liked to tell about students he had seen having sex in parked cars and you applied yourself to the U.S. Constitution and the separation of powers.

I got another job at the student radio station, WMMR, in October and a tall good-looking guy named Barry Halper showed me how to piece together a newscast from the Associated Press teletype. They needed someone to do the 12:15 newscast. "Today?" I said. "Today," he said. He showed me how to switch on the microphone, read the VU meter, adjust the headphone volume, showed me the cough switch, and an hour later I sat down in a tiny room with green acoustic-tile walls at a table covered with green felt and switched on the mike and a red bulb lit up and I read the news under a goose-neck lamp, one eye on the big clock on the wall in front of my face. I was nervous of course, but it was a delicious feeling. I felt sequestered, safe in the studio, a little fortress. I did the newscast and said, "That's the news, reported by Garrison Keillor. This is WMMR, from studios in Coffman Memorial Union, broadcasting at 730 kilocycles." And pressed a Play button and the tape deck clunked and a recorded voice talked about Campus Pizza and I got up and the next announcer slipped in and played something by Johnny Mathis and I walked out to the hall and Barry Halper nodded at me. "That was not bad," he said.

Barry told me I ought to go cover Kennedy's speech and I rode over to the Minneapolis Auditorium on a chartered bus that was packed, girls sitting on laps, boys crushed together in the aisle. I crushed myself into them and stood pressed against a girl's back, a solid mass of people swaying on the turns. I joined the crush streaming into the hall and climbed up under the rafters as the mighty Wurlitzer played "Happy Days Are Here Again" and sat through the prelims, all the little frogs getting their moment in the spotlight, and Senator Eugene

McCarthy was introduced and then Hubert, who got a long ovation but not too long, and then Orville Freeman got behind the lectern and introduced John F. Kennedy and out he came, covered in glory, and the place almost came loose from its moorings. In that shining moment, standing, grinning, drenched in applause, the whistles and the cheers, he truly seemed to rise to meet our hopes for him. I sort of knew the rap against him—he had dodged the issue of McCarthyism, his father's shady fortune had bought the nomination, the grandma of the Democratic Party, Eleanor Roosevelt, couldn't stand him because he wasn't Adlai Stevenson—but there in the flesh, he was thrilling to us Democrats, a plain people; he was the first politician with movie hero presence and he had the elegant dignity of someone who has always known who he is, unlike the herky-jerky Nixon of the mawkish Checkers speech and the weird marionette arms. Kennedy was classy, not overeager like so many politicians, who were tuned a half step sharp and didn't know how to play the crowd. They could do Earnest and Hortatory with the three obligatory jokes at the beginning and some Keening and Baying at the end and the Hands High Touchdown pose, but he had more keys on his piano. He had black keys and they didn't. There was playfulness in him; he didn't just preach about freedom, he performed it. (Did the GIs die in the snowy forests of Belgium so we could be like Nixon, the prisoner of his own demons? I didn't think so.)

Kennedy was a new man, a man of our time, not one of the old jowly guys who peered at TV cameras as if they were bombs and read from prepared texts and struck the old ritual poses, kissed the symbolic baby, ate the ceremonial hot dog, waved the flag, decried godless communism, posed with other jowly guys. Kennedy was an improviser. He stood there and grinned and soaked up the applause and then joked about Ted Williams having announced his retirement from the Red Sox at the age of 42—Kennedy was 43—"It shows that perhaps experience isn't enough." Huge laugh—and he tipped his hat to Hubert as a worthy opponent (more applause) and went on to his speech. I remember he quoted Dante—politicians didn't quote Dante then, any more than they'd pose in a little black beret with a cigarette dangling from their lower lip. Kennedy made you believe that at one time in his life he'd sat down and read the *Inferno,* that he lived in a house with books on the shelves and didn't care if you knew it, that he might have enjoyed Italy and knew about more than politics. He shared our disdain for the dull-witted bullies of the world who lord it over the meek and lowly. He was a liberating man. I didn't care that he was rich and Catholic. So what? It felt as if a great loosening was coming and a jazzier spirit was in the air. And we'd have a President for whom we felt admiration. So I was a Democrat. Republicans were those fraternity boys on University Avenue, the Dekes engaged in the manly pursuit of drunkenness and fart lighting, maintaining their antique Greek culture, the annual Pajama Parade and the Tunic Twirl where the frat houses sang their raccoon songs and Sno Week with the Lennon Sisters and the Glenn Miller Band on the bill, a bunch of glad-handers and blowhards, scions of car dealers, who devoted more attention to their hair than to what lay beneath it.

I walked back to campus from his speech. At 18, I was deeply into my family's history and I felt a connection between Kennedy and my family's New England roots, which I was just then hugely proud of, having recently learned about them. The reference to Dante was, "We have all made mistakes. But Dante tells us that divine justice weighs the sins of the cold-blooded and the sins of the warm-hearted on different scales. Better the occasional faults of a party living in the spirit of charity than the consistent omissions of a party frozen in the ice of its own indifference." To me this spoke volumes about the cold legalism of fundamentalist Christianity, which was its dark side—the bright side was the evangelical spirit and the gospel of Jesus Christ who came to free us from bondage—but then there was the cold literalist judgmental schismatic side and the gimlet-eyed blue-nosed martinets who would expel you into outer darkness if you departed from orthodoxy by so much as a quarter inch. My New England ancestors were warm-hearted. Joseph Crandall was an associate of Roger Williams who founded the first Baptist church in America in Providence in 1639. Roger Williams had grown up in England when Puritans were burned at the stake and came to Massachusetts Bay Colony where he found the Puritans to be just as intolerant as the people who had incinerated them back in England. He founded Rhode Island as a haven for people of all beliefs, including Indians. Roger Williams made Indian languages the great scholarly enterprise of his life. And my ancestor was there with him. And then there was Prudence Crandall who opened a school for young women in Canterbury, Connecticut, in 1831. When she admitted a colored girl the following year, all of the decent white families pulled their children out, whereupon Prudence opened a school for young colored women, the first in the country, which was shut down by a mob. She was a Quaker. She married a Baptist clergyman named Calvin Philleo and they moved to Kansas and she kept on teaching and was a staunch advocate of equal rights for women until she died in 1890. Mark Twain once spoke admiringly of Prudence Crandall and I was as proud of her as I could be, my ancestor who stood up to a mob for what she knew to be right. Maybe the rest of us Keillors were just clerks and farmhands and parking lot attendants but at one time we stood for something. So did Kennedy.

In the Great American Divide between the cold avengers and the sons of liberty, the paranoid and the happy entrepreneurs, the bullies and the defenders of justice, he was over on the side of the warm-hearted, and that was his mystique, no mystery about it.

I remember I walked in silence across that high narrow bridge over the Mississippi gorge and up the empty street behind Walter Library and thought about Kennedy and the Crandalls and the University and my ambitions to be a writer, which seemed to be all tangled up together in a ball, and was overjoyed a few weeks later when he beat Nixon. And then his heroic inauguration, his good speech with some nobility in it, and the heroic performance by Robert Frost of "The Gift Outright"—what a good country to be able to sense the difference between Nixon and Kennedy, even by a narrow margin. He stood in the light and he was worthy of our ideals. I never met him or his wife or children. I never was fascinated by their Kennedyness, only by him as President. Under his sway, I signed up for the Don Fraser for Congress campaign in 1962, which knocked off a crusty old Republican in Minneapolis and was managed by Don's wife Arvonne, a short peppery woman who personified for me the Democratic-Farmer-Labor party, open-hearted, perpetually hopeful, honest to a fault, and the mother of us all. I was in Eddy Hall on November 22, 1963, when I heard the President had been shot. I was an announcer at the University AM radio station, KUOM, and was sitting in the record library when the secretary, Bobbie, came in and told me. I walked to the United Press teletype in the hall closet and saw the first fragmentary bulletins, all caps, DALLAS, NOV. 22 (UPI)—THREE SHOTS WERE FIRED AT PRESIDENT KENNEDY'S MOTORCADE IN DOWN-TOWN DALLAS.—I stood reading this in stunned silence, the teletype clacking away, and there was something about the President's limp body being carried from the car, and the word *fatally* appeared, and I took the paper into the studio where an actor was reading Tolkien's *The Hobbit* on a show called *Your Novel*—he glanced up in alarm and I handed him the bulletin and he said, in a rather grand voice, "I have just been handed a news bulletin—" and I went back to the record library and got a record of, I think, a Spanish Mass and we played the *Benedictus*. And then Tchaikovsky's *Pathétique*. There was no need for us to read more news, everybody knew the news. Who killed him was never clear and either one read the conspiracy literature or one did not. I didn't. I never could bring myself to visit the assassination museum at the schoolbook depository in Dallas. Nothing I read later about Kennedy and his life essentially changed how I felt about him the night I walked back to campus from his speech in October 1960.

One day in the Scholar Coffeehouse, a kid strummed a 12-string guitar and everyone sang, without prompting, *Deep in my heart, I do believe that we shall overcome someday.* With all our hearts. Underneath the thin patina of coolness, we were all church kids. We'd read the prophets, heard the gospel, were exalted by the thought of being soldiers for the Lord and setting the prisoners free. Kennedy didn't live to see it, but it was done in his spirit.

A couple years after he died, the Mississippi River rose in the spring and there were urgent flood warnings on the radio. One afternoon I put on warm clothes and took the bus to St. Paul and crossed the Wabasha Bridge to the West Side where people were at work filling sandbags and building dikes to save the low-lying houses. It was foggy, and then it began to rain. An army of hundreds of volunteers hard at work, men and women, drawn up in assembly lines, holding the sacks and filling them and passing them in a chain to the dike. It got dark. Nobody left. The Red Cross brought around sandwiches and coffee. We rested and went back to work. Trucks brought in more sand and bags. A couple of front loaders worked at anchoring the dikes with earthen banks. It felt like wartime. I worked until after midnight and lay down in the back of a truck under a tarp and slept until daybreak

and got up stiff and cold and they brought us more sandwiches and coffee and I got back in the gang and worked
until noon. Someone said the flood would crest that
evening. Someone worried about the dike bursting. A
man said, "When they go, they go slow, they don't go
sudden." I wasn't sure about that, but I stayed because
everyone else stayed. I sort of collapsed in the afternoon
and was going to go home but slept a couple hours on a
tarp in somebody's front yard and when I woke up, there
was water in the street, people wading through it, some
men with muddy overalls, pitched emotion in the air,
though nobody said much. We had put so much into
beating back the flood, and we kept working— shovel,
fill, tie, and pass, shovel, fill, tie, and pass— and felt privileged to be there doing it. I could hear the river boiling by
and slabs of ice heaved up on the dike and National
Guardsmen patrolling and when people couldn't stand
up any longer, they sat down and ate baloney sandwiches
and drank coffee. And got back up.

I went home in the morning. It was so overwhelming,
I sat on the bed and cried. For the relief of getting out of
those mud-crusted clothes and standing under a hot
shower, but also for what I'd seen, the spirit of all those

workers caught up in the job of saving their neighbors' houses. Forget all the jabber and gossip, all the theoretical balderdash and horsefeathers, here is reality: the river rises up in its power and majesty, and the people rise up in theirs, and while one can do only so much, you must do that much, and we did. None of the news reports captured the reality of that event, which was the spirit of the crowd, of which I was one. An experience that warms a Democrat's heart, a scene from *Grapes of Wrath*, or the crossing of the Red Sea. The People, yes.

By God, no matter what Republicans say, the people of this country really do care about each other. We are not a cold people. By God, when John F. Kennedy said, "Ask what you can do for your country," he spoke to this country's heart and conscience.

My teachers Miss Story, Miss Melby, Mrs. Fleischman, Miss Hattendorf: those tireless encouragers and inspirers. They were children of the Depression who were impelled toward public service, a good career, and many of the women had grown up in large farm families and for them teaching was a shining ideal and also the path out of a hard life they knew too well, the life of serfs. The very word *education* was dazzling to them, and they marched off to earn their way through teachers' college and put on starched collars and pick up pointers and point. How beautiful is the life of the mind to those who know about doing laundry by hand and pressing the clothes with a hot iron from a woodstove and hauling buckets of water for the baths. Miss Hattendorf grew up on a farm in Iowa; her German parents sent her and her sisters to board with a family in town so they could attend high school. When Miss Hattendorf was about to leave for the University of Chicago and it came time to say goodbye and get in the car and go to the train, she looked at her mother standing at the kitchen sink—"I wanted to hug her, but I couldn't do it. She was a stranger to me. They wanted me and my sisters to get a good education and they made big sacrifices and that was one of them: they didn't know us anymore and we didn't know them."

There are many stories of sacrifice and idealism like hers—and one of the dark deeds of the Republican anarchists is their denigration of public service and their characterization of public servants as parasites, busybodies, incompetents. To the cheater, there is no such thing as honesty, and to Republicans the idea of serving the public good is counterfeit on the face of it—they never felt such an urge, therefore it must not exist. But John F. Kennedy knew it and gave voice to it.

Chapter 6

THE SPIRIT OF EQUALITY

I often think of John Kennedy.
After years in the U.S. Senate, he
Became Chief Executive,
Then like Thomas Becket of
England found sudden serenity.

JOHN F. KENNEDY made a big impression on me, but attending the University was what confirmed me as a Democrat, the thought that the taxpayers of Minnesota really had faith that knowledge and understanding ennoble us. An egalitarian spirit prevailed at the U that truly was noble. There was no rank, no hazing, no freshman beanies, we were all in the same boat. You were Mr. Keillor to your professor and he was Mr. Brown to you. You looked him in the eye. You said, "I don't get this" and he explained it to you. That was his job. Yours was to pay attention. Money was no social asset whatsoever and if you went around in expensive clothes you were regarded with pity or scorn. A few goofball freshmen showed up in brand new suits for fall classes and they stood out in the crowd as if they wore red rubber noses and fright wigs. Everybody from the President to the deans and the faculty had their home addresses and phone numbers listed in the University directory, and if you were brave enough, you could ring up Dean McDiarmid or Vice President Willey and tell him your troubles. I did not but the phone numbers were there and I suppose somebody did. On my slender parking lot wages I was able to buy a season ticket to the concerts in Northrup and I saw Isaac Stern, Arthur Rubinstein, Andrés Segovia, the Royal Danish Ballet doing a Balanchine program, the great Swedish tenor Jussi Bjoerling, the Cleveland Orchestra, Glenn Gould—you could get a balcony seat for $1.50, about an hour's wage. I couldn't afford to see the Metropolitan Opera on their annual tour but one evening I did look up at a window on the side of Northrup and see a tall slender dark-haired woman standing naked in front of a full-length mirror for a whole minute, studying herself. A wardrobe lady sat nearby, smoking, reading a newspaper. The dark-haired woman turned, facing me, her hands on hips, one leg extended, looking over her shoulder at her rump, her delicate bush and maroon nipples, like a painting, NUDE DANCER STUDYING HERSELF.

Robert Frost came to campus soon after Kennedy's speech and drew a capacity crowd of 5,000 at Northrup Auditorium, the great stooped white-maned old bear reciting by heart "Stopping by Woods on a Snowy Evening" and the crowd hushed in the cathedral of poetry—"For Once, Then, Something" and "The Oven Bird" and "Fire and Ice" and the one about the lover's quarrel with the world—that soft lyrical cranky uncle voice beloved since junior high, a godlike presence in our midst, and afterward a hundred of us acolytes gathered at the back door to view the great man up close. I was proud of him for drawing that huge crowd and performing so well. He eased his old body down the stairs, our grand paterfamilias, and mingled with us, chatted, answered a few questions—I remember clearly, nobody asked for his autograph—and then he climbed into a black Chrysler and was taken off to lunch with the faculty. But we students were as important as anybody else and weren't held behind ropes or shushed. That was how it was at the U. The field was wide open. At the Minnesota *Daily* and its literary arm, *The Ivory Tower,* you submitted your stuff and back came a polite note, "Sorry," and that week they printed George Amabile's poems instead of yours, but you sent more and of that second batch the editor accepted two and the next month they appeared, big glutinous symbolist things about owls on moonless nights flying to Arabia, all in lowercase, and you snatched ten copies out of a paper box and took them home to save to show your grandchildren you once were a writer. The publications weren't in the grip of a gang, they were open to walk-ons.

College. The only time in your life when you can be gloriously ridiculously full of yourself and get away with it. A luxury once reserved for the aristocracy, now extended to the children of postal workers. I was a middleclass kid from the West River Road where late at night fireflies sparkled in the field behind the dark houses with blue TV light flickering and the rich green moist lawns and the great harmonic of green and white houses and black asphalt and ten miles south on the Mississippi I found the University where I could imagine a larger life and hope to escape the downdraft of the suburbs and do what I loved to do, write, though it seemed presumptuous. I secretly imagined getting published in *The New Yorker.* I hung around the *Daily* offices, free of the petty miseries of high school, that small fixed universe. The University was freedom. A friend of mine dropped out sophomore year and married his girlfriend and they bought a little yellow rambler in Coon Rapids, the down payment a gift from her parents. He was a warehouse clerk and his wife got pregnant and woke up in a foul mood every morning and he went off to eight hours of an automaton job. What a waste of a perfectly good life. Women were the great tamers; they took you in hand and trained you to accept the leaden social life and waxen solemnity of marriage and instead of bumming around Europe you'd be spending two weeks with her parents at the lake. Women put their arms around you and cried that they loved you and wanted to make you happy and *bwanngggg* a trapdoor popped open and you dropped down the chute into a job you despised and a frazzled marriage in a crackerjack house with a mortgage as big as Montana—I intended to escape that. I longed for my flesh to touch someone else's flesh but I remained chaste. I sat in clouds of cigarette smoke in a classroom smelling of linseed-oiled floors and listened to James Wright lecture on Dickens and gazed at the lovely girls in horn-rim glasses. I liked strolling around campus at night with Gail who wrote for the paper or my classmate Mary, put my arm around her waist and hooked my little finger in her belt loop and she with her arm around the back of me, hooked together, talking about Chaucer, Shakespeare, Eliot, arms riding across each other's butts, our hips moving in meter, which, we two being different heights, came out in 9/7 time, like an old Swedish step dance, and I would maybe recite Housman's poem about being 20—"And take from seventy springs a score,/It only leaves me fifty more./And since to look at things in bloom/Fifty springs are little room,/About the woodlands I will go/To see the cherry hung with snow"—and wind up back at Murphy Hall and the *Daily* office.

For winter quarter, I got the 5 A.M. shift at a ten-acre gravel parking lot on the West Bank, overlooking the Mississippi. I was turning into a night owl, always up past midnight, and the alarm clock went off at 4 and I lay in the warm trench of my bed, reviewing my options, preferring sleep, longed for it, nodded off, which shocked me into wakefulness and I rolled out and drove to town through the snowy world and parked beside the parking lot shack and hiked to the far end of the lot, flashlight in hand, like a sheep shearer waiting for the herd to come piling through the gate. The lot sloped down to the edge of the bluff and I looked down on Bohemian Flats, a ragtag village on the riverbank. Old frame houses that got flooded out every spring, where old Swedes and Bohunks lived a subsistence life in the middle of the Twin Cities. Smoke rose from their chimneys. One of the other parking attendants said there was a whorehouse down there. "Ten bucks a shot," he said. "Indian women." I got good at parking. The cars came in a rush, starting at 6:30. Three ticket sellers stood in the street, and the flagman stood at the top of the lot and directed the flow to where I was conducting them into their spots, straight lines, double rows. No painted lines on the gravel, I did it all by eye.

I had to direct each car with strong hand signals into its correct space, the Otto Klemperer of the automobile, and discourage the tendency to freelance and veer off toward a more convenient place. Every morning there were three or four pioneers who wanted to start their own rows. You had to yell to the flagman to hold the traffic and then you ran over toward the miscreant's car and yelled "Your car will be towed in ten minutes." The mention of towing got their attention, but you had to make it sound real. "That's a twenty-five-dollar fine." Usually that was enough to get them to move the car. If they hesitated, I said, "Plus twenty-five for the impound lot. It's up to you." I had no idea who to call to come tow a car or what they would say, I just did what other attendants said to do, and it worked. Creative parking couldn't be allowed, chaos would result, cars skewed everywhere, blocking other cars, holding up traffic, people late, angry, honking—it was my responsibility to make the grid system work. For the common good. To be direct. Exercise authority. **No, sir. Not there. Over here. Right here. Yes. Here.** Your individualists and comedians would test the limits and if you gave them an inch, anarchy would ensue, cars going every which way like confused buffalo. Be firm. Make that bozo back up six inches. Straighten that line. Thank you. If you accept that variance, the line will buckle. If you do your job right, the lot fills to capacity in half an hour, you put up the FULL sign and huddle in the shack, the electric heater blazing away, and you take up with Natasha and Prince Andrei and *War and Peace* for Mr. Milgrom's humanities class until 9 A.M. when the shift ends and you leg it over the Washington Avenue bridge to the East Bank. A cup of vending machine coffee and a cheese danish and off to class.

In the winter, we packed into Williams Arena to cheer the hockey team against our deadly rival, the Fighting Sioux of North Dakota. Blood lust in the air. Our Gophers were all Minnesota boys and the Sioux were all Canucks, paid thugs, big bruisers, mercenaries, and when a Sioux got ridden into the boards, we cheered from the bottom of our hearts. I dated a quiet girl, a church organist, and at hockey games she screeched and booed like a true peasant. I wrote a poem about hockey and took it to a writers' club meeting at Professor Hage's house and the poet James Wright said something encouraging about it and my face burned with pleasure. I can still picture it in my mind, where I was sitting, where he sat, and I still feel my face getting warm.

The University was a monument to the Jeffersonian faith in the power of learning and in the ability of all people to recognize and embrace excellence, a grand old American notion. To offer Jussi Bjoerling and Arthur

Rubinstein to 18-year-old kids at prices they can afford is an astonishment. Utterly. To witness such grandeur can change a person's life. But that was the spirit of the Morrill Act of 1862 that granted to the states a tract of land in proportion to their population for the endowment of a state university to teach the classic curriculum as well as courses relating to agriculture and industry, open to qualified students regardless of financial means. I paid $71 tuition for a quarter at the U, and today, U of M students pay about $6,000 for a year's tuition, which is $2,000 for what cost me $71, which says a lot about politics today. Tuition has been cranked up as the classic curriculum is doinked around with and class sizes go up and the idea of excellence is abandoned, a heartless way to welcome the next generation, to sell them a cardboard car for ten times the money.

My Latin teacher, Margaret Forbes, was an auntly woman, cheery and kind, who ran us through daily translations and sniped at us with questions about the anticipatory subjunctive—subjunctive denotes an act that is expected—*Expectabum dum frater redirect*—I was waiting for my brother to return—and we responded to her *aequo animo*—without anxiety, as she lay open the folded language—*patefacio, patefacere, patefeci, patefactum—O pace in perpetuum*, Margaret, *felicitas aeternas*! Richard Cody taught composition, a slender Englishman sitting at a table on a raised platform, lecturing drily on the art of the essay, which he described as a 440-yard dash through natural obstacles, over rough terrain, an intellectual exercise also meant to be esthetically elegant. We were Minnesota kids striving to imitate William Hazlitt, Joseph Addison, George Orwell, E. B. White, and Norman Mailer. Once Mr. Cody called on me to come forward and read the first page of my essay on manure spreading, one of my jobs on Uncle Jim's farm—a humorous essay, supposedly—and I jumped up to do it and fainted dead away—fell across a row of empty chairs and crashed to the floor and lay there. "Are you all right?" a girl asked under her breath. I got up and Mr. Cody called on someone else. We were all pretty cool back then. Asher Christiansen taught American Government, an elegant little man in dark slacks and gray blazer, bushy eyebrows, moustache, smoking his pipe—half the class smoked too, and I came to associate intellectual seriousness with bad air—propounding his grand theme, that the Constitution was a natural force for civilization, its checks and balances serving to dampen the fires of inner-directed ideologues and bring them into a respectful relationship to their antagonists and attend to the serious business of government. After class, some students formed another smaller class that followed Professor Christiansen out the door and stood in the alley behind Nicholson Hall for a few minutes, a gaggle of fifteen or twenty that dwindled as he headed down the Mall to his office in Ford Hall, arriving there with four or five of us still hanging on. I was a student in the last class he taught. In January I saw the front-page story in the *Daily:* Professor Christiansen had felt ill during lunch at the faculty club and went to a quiet room to lie down and died there of a heart attack. The story said he grew up in Little Falls, graduated from the U, where he taught from 1936 on, with guest stints in Wales, Germany, and Argentina, where he lectured in Spanish. He was 57 years old, married, no children. Just us students.

I stuck around at WMMR and did the noon newscast for six months, five days a week, and then in May was told that the station had been off the air for at least that long. Doggone it. Our engineer, a brilliant young man, had been busy building a state-of-the-art control room and hadn't had time to do maintenance on the transmitter and it had burned out. I was in some anguish over having spent six months editing a newscast so I could sit in a room and read it to myself, but as Barry Halper said, "It was good experience." And had I ever, in those six months, thought about the listeners and wondered why the cards and letters weren't pouring in, or trickling in, or even dripping in? No. I was having too much fun. "You sound terrific," said Barry. "You could get a job on any station in town." He was a pal and a real positive guy. He was 20, he drove a big white convertible, he was Jewish and smart, he'd been to LA and Las Vegas and met Jack Benny and Shelley Berman. If he'd asked me to, I would've shined his shoes.

I was a serious young man and did not go to parties at the U except one in the spring of my sophomore year at somebody's parents' house in Kenwood, a tony neighborhood in Minneapolis, where a mob of students was drinking something called Purple Death out of a washtub in the kitchen. Fortified with this, people started spouting off their big opinions about Kennedy and Hemingway and Ornette Coleman and some of us got into a contest to see who knew more dirty limericks. There was the one about the young man from Buckingham and the young man from St. Paul whose cock was exceedingly small and the Bishop of Chichester and the sailor named Tex who avoided premarital sex and the young woman of Edina and her vagina.

The base of Purple Death was grape Kool-Aid, plus whatever the guests had brought. It was a potluck cocktail: Old Buzzard Breath bourbon, crème de banana, licorice schnapps, vodka, anything would do, and after drinking for a while and telling dirty jokes, some of us headed over to Cedar Lake to go skinny-dipping, and we stripped off our clothes, but it wasn't the erotic thrill it should've been, not for me anyway: I could feel the hangover mounting up behind my forehead, a truly monumental one, with shades of surrealism—I remember naked women and I also remember the dark angel of projectile vomiting—and in the morning I awoke with a taste of what mental illness might be like, a sort of vacancy with dark shadows. And I was glad to be alone.

As U of M students we walked around with a fine chip on our shoulder toward eastern finishing schools like Yale and Harvard where children of privilege slept until noon after a night of inebriation, were brought cucumber sandwiches by a porter, sashayed off to their 3 P.M.

music appreciation class, and then played squash until dinner. Oxford and Cambridge were held in even greater contempt: dandruffy men quivering with borrowed sensibility drinking sherry and propounding fabulous foolishness with great certainty. You walk around with a brown bag lunch and a few bucks in your pocket, trying to scrape together next quarter's tuition, and a little class resentment is good for you, a balm and a prod both. I envied cool people, good tennis players, opera singers, sandy-haired rich guys who looked princely even in ratty old clothes, all Frenchmen, men with lovely girlfriends, guitarists, but the U was the antidote to envy. So many cool people seem on closer examination to be trapped in a set of mannerisms that are not so interesting and lead nowhere, whereas the U appealed to your curiosity and drew you into scholarship, which took you through doors you hadn't known existed. In one smoky classroom after another, sitting elbow to elbow at little arm desks, you felt illuminated, there was a quickening almost like drunkenness, a feeling that you and the professor were conspiring in a noble enterprise that would last you to the end of your days. I learned how to plant myself in a library chair and open the books and take notes in a yellow legal pad. Having a good ear for multiple-choice tests had gotten me through high school (the correct answer, two-thirds of the time, was C) but now I needed to actually do the work. I soldiered through and learned how to write profoundly at great speed late at night about books I barely understood.

American universities have seen plenty of radicals and revolutionaries come and go over the years, and all of them put together were not nearly so revolutionary as a land-grant university itself on an ordinary weekday. To give people with little money a chance to get the best education there is—that is true revolution. When I graduated from Anoka High School, I believed that my chances would be as good as anybody else's, and the good people of Minnesota did not let me down. I got my chance and right there is where a Democrat is made—a kid from Anoka sits in a parking lot shack on Fourth Street SE where, earning $1.48 an hour, he translates Horace for Mrs. Forbes—whose standards are high—as birds sit scritching on the telephone wire and a fly buzzes at the window. A bright fall day and he has no money to speak of and no clear plan for the future but he has teachers who engage him with gravity and fervor and that's enough. That was the true spirit of the University, the spirit of professors who loved their work. That was the heart and soul of the place, not the athletic teams, not the architecture. The University was Mary Malcolm, a native of Worthington, who studied in Paris with Nadia Boulanger and came back to teach music theory for forty-three years. She had perfect pitch and could write down on paper anything you could hum or plunk on the piano. It was Izaak M. Kolthoff, a Dutch chemist who guided Jewish scientists out of Germany in the Thirties and worked on the crucial war project of creating synthetic rubber and became a peacenik in the Fifties. It was Marcia Edwards, a chain-smoking authority on adolescent psychology and a fanatical Gopher sports fan who went to angelic lengths to help her students, even lending them money, and who turned down the offer to become dean of the College of Education because she didn't want the hassle, especially the foofaraw of being the first woman dean. It was Bill Marchand who taught Shakespeare to kids majoring in animal husbandry and horticulture. It was Nils Hasselmo who came from Sweden to study the Swedish emigrants and got his doctorate and became chair of the Scandinavian Languages

Department and eventually President of the U. And it was Margaret Forbes who could make you feel that a few lines of Horace held the key to everything noble. And if you start to feel ennobled, you lose interest in how you are perceived by other people. You walk into the library and that Niagara of scholarship holds you in its sway, the deluge and glory of learning, and you begin to see where work and play become one. And imagine working at something you love. And that was how the University of Minnesota gave me my life.

Chapter 7

REAL LIVES,
REAL CONSEQUENCES

There was a young teacher named Seth
Who often said, under his breath,
When besieged by the tots,
Various thoughts
One associates with Lady Macbeth.

WE DEMOCRATS are deeply flawed people, but we do stick to our guns, and believe in decency and public spiritedness and have refused to hitch our wagon to yahooism and intolerance and have supported government as a necessary force for good to "establish justice, ensure domestic tranquility, provide for the common defence, promote the general welfare, and secure the blessings of liberty . . ."

We can be perfectly and sweetly corrupt—I think

97

back to the logrolling I witnessed at the National Endowment for the Arts, petty politics at work to bestow public largesse on the projects of one's pals—and Lord knows we can be earnestly boring. Oh God. We sermonize about the Unmet Needs of the elderly urban Indian and the dyslexic lesbian and the emotionally disadvantaged Estrogen-American and we promise the moon on a string and it bores the eyeballs right out of people. We can be awfully righteous about moral issues in faraway places: we tend to see more clearly at a distance and to love humanity in the abstract and care less about individuals. We take perverse pleasure in seeing tycoons in handcuffs, we enjoy the banality of the Trumps and the Bushes and the Hiltons, their proud illiteracy, their simple love of the garish, their air-conditioned nightmare. We can take a good high-school course like world geography and change it to Frameworks of Belonging and, instead of teaching kids where Switzerland is, have them write about feeling lost and disconnected. We can be weenies, masters of rinky-dink. We can stand up and argue that *dyslexic* is a marginalizing term and *paralexic* is better, that wrong answers are not *wrong*, but rather *alternative* views of the world. We tend to be revisionists and dissenters and boycotters and quick to re-sign in protest. *The Democrat was shipwrecked on a desert island for years and lived there alone and finally he was rescued and he showed the rescue party around the island. He said, "See there, I built myself a house over there. And over there is my barn. And that building over there is my church." And the rescue party said, "And what's that building back there?" "Oh," he said. "That. That's the church I used to go to."* We took some wrong turns in the past when we swung away from the bread-and-butter AFL-CIO issues and into symbolic stuff like the ERA. We are profoundly indecisive, nervous about strong emotion, reluctant to invoke the Deity, susceptible to the vapors like a herd of turkeys liable to panic at lightning and stampede into a fence and pile up and suffocate. We are capable of doing dumb things in the name of the common good and sponsoring National Self-Awareness Week and print up brochures reminding people not to walk into open manholes. We have a weakness for rule making to ensure that nothing bad can happen, which leads us into thickets that go nowhere anybody needs to go. A world that is perfectly safe from sexual harassment is a world without flirtation. A world with airtight protection against thieves will have no entrepreneurs. And a world without fiction would be unbearable for all of us. Once, at a party in St. Paul, I heard a woman talk at some length about diversity and how persons of "noncolor" should not impose their majority culture on others and the phrase *persons of noncolor*— the idea of being colorless—made me reach for my coat and hat. *Goodbye, I'm out of here. Call me when you get over it.*

We Democrats are at our worst when we lose touch with our principles—the protection of the powerless, paying attention to real consequences in the lives of real people and not flying on slogans or glib phrases—and we try to emulate Republicans as we did in signing onto the "war" on drugs that has ruined so many young lives. In our nation's capital, nearly 50% of black men between 18 and 35 are either in prison or on probation or parole—nationally, it's a human disaster: 6.6 million Americans in prison, nearly half of whom are black men. The cruelty of the Sentencing Reform Act of 1984 is stark indeed, and of sentencing guidelines that impose mandatory minimum sentences for minor drug possession—guidelines in the 1986 Anti-Drug Abuse

Act that sailed through Congress without benefit of public hearings, drafted before an election by Democrats afraid to be labeled "soft on drugs"—and so a marijuana grower can land in prison for life without parole while a murderer might be in for eight years: no rational person can defend this, it is a Dostoevskian nightmare and it exists only because politicians fled in the face of danger. That includes Bill Clinton, under whose administration the prosecution of Americans for marijuana went up hugely so that now there are more folks in prison for marijuana than for violent crimes. More than for manslaughter or rape. This only makes sense in the fantasy world of Washington, where perception counts for more than reality. To an old Democrat, who takes a ground view of politics—*What is the actual effect of this action on the lives of real people?*—it is a foul tragedy that makes you feel guilty about enjoying your freedom. Here I am, drinking coffee in a café in St. Paul and tolerating this shameful savagery in our midst. If the State cuts off your right hand with a meat cleaver on my account and I don't object, then it is my cleaver and my fingerprints on it. I don't dare visit Sandstone Federal Prison for fear of what I'd see there. People who chose marijuana, a more benign drug than alcohol, and got caught in the religious war that we Democrats in a weak moment signed on to. God help us if we form alliance with such bullies as would destroy a kid's life for raising cannabis plants.

Nonetheless, for all I can say against Democrats, we are the party that upholds the generous spirit even when we ourselves are mean. We are the party that respects the individual, believing that each American is complicated, poetic, full of mystery and genius, capable of profound love, also capable of meanness, which makes it important for politics to be charitable lest we unleash the mob. This is never far away, the crowds with torches howling for the Jews, or blacks, or Mormons, or Japanese.

I became a Democrat because I was eager and hopeful, not because I was angry. Anger makes for amusing radio shows but it's got a short shelf life. It's a crummy way to live. Your mother was right: forgive and forget. Live in the present and you'll be happier. Your old bachelor uncle Art who camps in his easy chair grumbling about the New Deal and how the Depression was a hoax and anybody who wanted to work could get a job but no, the gummint came in with its WPA (We Poke Along) to reward the indolent, and Pearl Harbor was arranged by that drunken womanizer Roosevelt to get us into the war and we shouldn't have been fighting Hitler anyway, Stalin was the real enemy, which you wouldn't know from reading the papers because they're all owned by Jews—you wouldn't want this dear man to be put in charge of anything that matters. Let him wave a flag at the Fourth of July parade, but don't let him give a speech and embarrass your kids. And don't put him in charge of the lunch: leave that to people who can run things. In Minnesota we had an angry skinhead governor named Jesse (The Body) Ventura who slouched into office on 37% of the vote and turned out to be an opportunist whose first act in office was to sell the book rights. He was a troubled soul, thin-skinned, a growler and ranter and snit thrower. After four years of him it was a relief to go back to politics as usual, where soft-spoken people with ordinary chest sizes sit down and negotiate and get the job done. He was a professional wrestler, used to working within a simple story structure, but politics isn't a story, it's a process. It's not about confrontation and threat and revenge and triumph. It's mostly about civility. Most men and women in politics are there because they genuinely care about people and want to do good things in their behalf. Most people who ever saw it up close came away impressed.

WHAT DO-GOODER DEMOCRATS HAVE DONE FOR YOU

*

Civil Rights. In 1960, when I entered college, there was a whole large swath of America where white people and black people had to be careful how they mingled and what they said to each other. Colored passengers sat in the rear and white passengers in the front in cities all across the South. The drinking fountains, the schools, the churches, the polling places, American apartheid evident everywhere. People marched in the streets to claim the right to vote and faced state troopers who stormed them with clubs and tear gas. And when the marchers sang "We Shall Overcome," simple decency told you to sing with them. At the Democratic National Convention of 1948, Hubert Humphrey had spoken out for civil rights and provoked Strom Thurmond, the segregationist and father of a child by a young black servant of his family, to walk out and take a hike to the Republican Party where he truly belonged.

Jimmy Carter was prospering in Plains, Georgia, and owned a fertilizer plant and a peanut shellery and warehouses, and then the White Citizens Council pressured him to join their crusade and boycotted him when he refused, which stuck in his craw and got him interested in running for governor. He didn't like to be pushed around by arrogant guys who poke a finger in your sternum and tell you what to think. Like the colonial ancestors who got pushed and poked by the royal governors and then started to poke back.

The Sixties was a watershed time for Republicans: they seized a great political opportunity and shoved Abraham Lincoln into the closet and took up Stephen Douglas's flag of states' rights ("I care more for the great principle of self-government . . . and the great inalienable rights of white men . . . than I do for all the Negroes in Christendom"), which carried the Republicans to power in one national election after another. What exactly it is that Republicans have done for the South other than wave the flag and the Bible, I don't quite fathom.

Girls with Ponytails. A girl today can look forward to a life of such opportunity as her old grandmother wouldn't have dared imagine back in 1960. Betty Friedan did her part along with other big brassy women, the 1963 Presidential Commission on the Status of Women recognized the fact of sex discrimination, and in 1972, Congress passed Title IX legislation making it illegal to discriminate against women in employment and in education, including sports, and from this came the legions of lean girls with ponytails tearing around the basketball courts and soccer fields of America. The self-confidence and discipline and physical joy of sports were not so available to the girls I went to high school with. Girls who loved games beyond puberty were thought to be odd, mannish, unattractive. Today, you see dads in the bleachers who jump up and cheer their daughters more fervently than dads ever dared to cheer their sons, with great depths of feeling, Republican or Democrat— American dads have become feminists in behalf of their daughters, a tidal change for which you should thank the Democratic Party, like it or not. Girls who aren't feminists have risen on the same tide as girls who are, the southern Baptist confederate Republican girls of Charlotte and Birmingham have risen along with the leftist granola girls of Cambridge and Berkeley. The women who agitated for sexual equality and the men who listened to them first were Democrats. Republicans would have been content to have the ladies make lunch and be winsome and deferential. Thanks to Democrats, your daughter can think about going to medical school or pushing off into the corporate shark tank or choice C or D or E, and the world seems more normal with women circulating freely in it. Young women today don't tiptoe around men or avert their eyes like vestal virgins; they speak up and expect to be heard. Men and women mingle more or less unself-consciously as equals and a man who cannot deal with this is considered definitely weird.

Clean Air. No-smoking laws: a major intrusion by do-gooders into people's lives, and pity the poor office workers huddled in doorways smoking, but almost everyone sees it as a step forward, away from the smoky class-rooms and offices of my youth, and a kindness to us all. I smoked Luckies and Pall Malls, three packs a day for twenty years, and quit before the posse arrived, a good thing because I would have *hated* being sent outdoors to smoke, but in the end, I would have gone, grousing and complaining, and eventually quit. They say you can't legislate behavior, and maybe you can't, but you sure can give it a push in the right direction. Or so Democrats believe.

Geezerhood. If we're lucky, we get old, and there is more dignity in old age today, thanks to Medicare. Ask my mother: she's 88 and lives in her old home among her mementos, putting one foot ahead of the other, stubbornly independent, whereas her father languished in a nursing home in his old age and saw his savings dribble away and died at 73. She has arthritis and various other ailments, and life is diminished on account of them—she doesn't drive a car or garden (except for the plants on her deck) or whomp up big dinners and she takes great care navigating a snowy sidewalk—but life is pretty good. She sits in her old living room and looks out at the lawn that was a cornfield when Dad dug the basement in 1947 and built the house board by board and planted spindly trees that grew into a grove of giants, where her six little kids tore around and where a solid double off the bat of cousin Don smashed the picture window in the summer of 1954. Fifty Christmas trees have stood in that corner of the living room. Dozens of children in graduation gowns were photographed in this room. Grandbabies were brought here to be adored. Dad died in the downstairs bedroom. And one large cornerstone in her life is Medicare, which, for the grand sum of $58.70 a month, gives her quick access to physicians, a visit to the emergency room if need be, even a trip to the Mayo Clinic to see why she is feeling so fatigued these days. She ran up about $5,000 in medical bills last year of which she paid only $146.

I would gladly pay her bills but then she'd need to involve me in her decisions and would lose some of her privacy, a precious thing to my mother, who went through a rough time fighting off colon cancer and chose not to say much about it. If I were her benefactor, she would feel she was a burden. It is so much simpler and better for everyone to simply say: old people have a right to health care and that's that.

Medicare is the creation of Democrats and it has changed old age. If you're old, you aren't expected to accept pain and misery as your cross to bear and sit quietly by the window and sink uncomplaining into the dark. You're allowed to feel you can totter off to a clinic and claim the attention of a doctor and recite your complaints and hope to feel better. "I have trouble breathing. My knees hurt." *Well, let's have a look.* If you're 90 and really hoping for five more good years, we'll do what we can for you. Maybe you can have ten. If you're depressed, ask your doctor about drugs, and if you need help to function sexually, ask about that. Even if you're 80. This is new. Medicare says that even though you're not working and may need special help with the ordinary business of life, nonetheless you have value in this society. This is a Democratic idea. Be a howling right-winger if it gives you pleasure, but nonetheless milk comes from cows and Medicare comes from Democrats.

Pregnant Teens. Legal abortion is due to *Roe v. Wade*, not to Democrats, but we have defended it, even those of us with moral reservations about it. As the teen pregnancy rate declines and the abortion rate along with it, we can see the day approaching when this angry issue recedes, and we pro-choice Democrats can reconcile with our natural allies in the Catholic Church. The Church is morally offended by abortion and it is also offended by poverty and social injustice in ways that Republicans never could be: to oppose abortion, as they do, and also promote low wages and harass welfare mothers and hack away at public services—this is moral dishonesty that staggers the mind. This is stepping on the drowning woman's hand as she grabs onto the gunwale.

As long as we have pregnant girls of 12 and 13 and 14, there will be abortion. For them, and for others, the prospect of parenthood is grim beyond words. A 13-year-old girl is too young to be a mother, and if she is living in poverty with an angry drug-addled mother of her own, she doesn't stand much chance of bringing up a healthy child and having any decent life herself. So, rather than leave her to suffer the consequences of her behavior, we allow the drastic and merciful step of abortion of the embryo. The pro-lifers who demonstrate at Planned Parenthood clinics and hold up pictures of bloody fetuses should rather hold up signs with the number of hours per week they're volunteering for child care, and then we'd take them more seriously.

We live in a culture that so exploits sexuality that little kids grow up in a red-light district, even suburban and small town kids. Kids get wired early on into sexual roles, girls of 9 and 10 dress like streetwalkers, and it isn't left-wing academics who are selling this to them, it is corporate America, and it's the symbiotic link between puritans and pornographers (similar to that between prohibitionists and bootleggers) that makes the game go round. Janet Jackson's right tit, exposed on national TV at the Super Bowl, was the talk of the nation, more in bemusement—after all, the woman had products to promote—but the usual voices of shock and dismay were raised, thus raising the promotional value. Why do Republicans not get this? Their sulfurous views about sex, their obsession over it make the prize more attractive, and so, in the United States, girls under 15 are at least five times more likely to get pregnant than girls the same age in Old Europe where sex is viewed as an ordinary part of life and nothing to huff and puff about. A little secularism might help. If your daughter were 15 and pregnant, scared to death, weeping, angry at herself, embarrassed, you would do whatever you had to do to do right by her. You would not send her to the Rev. Falwell. You would not throw her to the winds to drift into depression and despair and deliver her child in a toilet and leave it in a Dumpster to die. And you wouldn't want anybody else's daughter to drift that way either.

Oddballs. Mental illness is not the shameful secret it used to be—if you suffer from depression, if you're alcoholic, if you have an autistic child, you can look other people in the eye and say so and expect them to be decent about it. You just say, "I'm bipolar," or "My son is schizophrenic," or "My daughter has apraxia," and that is that. "Oh," they say, and you talk about it, or you don't, and life goes on. This can't be chalked up to Democrats, but it should be on the list of civilities. Yes, the country has swung too far toward confessionalism, but mental illness needs to be named and acknowledged so it can be accepted and put in its proper place and life can go on. I often think of Lonnie and Ronnie and Dorby who went to grade school with me, and who were different, slower, more lumpish—we didn't know what was wrong, nobody said, we weren't supposed to ask—and then, somewhere in junior high school, they simply vanished. Where did they go? What was their problem? Nobody would say it out loud. Things are different now.

Cops. Law enforcement is better. Way better. Cops are more likely to be trained professionals and not bullies in a uniform. They look more like us and less like a Moose lodge. Those old bull elephants are gone who liked to swagger up to a carful of teenagers and make them get out and poke them in the chests and threaten them. The Iowa state patrolman who pulled me over late one night years ago, told me to get out and lie facedown on the shoulder of the road while he radioed my license plate number to headquarters, and twenty minutes later told me to get up and get the hell out. My offense—I knew it and he knew that I knew it—was that I had long hair. That sort of cop is gone. In St. Paul, if your car has been broken into, you get prompt service: the officer comes to your door, fills out the forms, gives you some tips on prevention, and gives you a cop's view of what's going on in the neighborhood these days. You feel well served. The result is greater respect for the law, which is just common sense: that's our badge on their chests, our lives and property that hang in the balance. Republicans have a dark urge to privatize the police, which is yet one more of their disastrous ideas: law enforcement is not a business, it is a calling, a pure public service. Sensible Democrats know this.

Tolerance. Make fun of p.c. to your heart's content, but there is less outright cruelty toward the vulnerable in everyday life. All the ramps that got carved into curbs at intersections, according to federal specs in the Americans with Disabilities Act of 1990, for people in wheelchairs, (also a boon to parents pushing strollers and kids on bikes): that's new, a little monument to sensitivity. The ADA, like the gay rights movement, was built on the women's movement, which was built on the civil rights movement which gave us the Civil Rights Act of 1964, a large moment in American history. In my youth, you heard respectable men tell jokes about Hebes and Yids and coons and niggers, and then came the Montgomery bus boycott and Greensboro and the first sit-in, February 1, 1960, and things changed. Not everything, but some things. Decent people don't wink at racism anymore. The country is more tolerant. Gay men and women are neighbors, friends, relatives. When I was a kid, our Boy Scout troop sent a basketball team to play a black team at Phyllis Wheatley settlement house in north Minneapolis, and it was rather dramatic to us Anoka kids. They were *Negroes*. All of them. Black. It was something of a Large Gesture of Brotherhood on our part. Today it would just be fun.

*

There is racism still, but not so implacable, it can be worked around, teased, poked, prodded. Most Americans feel there is something screwy about a person who can't relate to his fellow humans of any color. This is in the American tradition of tolerance going back to 1654, when the Dutch of New Amsterdam forbade public worship except in the Dutch Reformed Church, but when a shipload of Jews arrived from Brazil and held the first Rosh Hashanah service, the authorities said, *Well, all right. Go ahead. It's no skin off my nose. Whatever. It's a big country. Who am I to judge?* That's the American spirit. Republicans don't seem to understand that.

*

These changes toward a civil society were aided and abetted by government—government big enough to have impact, with a capable bureaucracy to work patiently through cumbersome due process and accomplish incremental change—all done, not out of anger but for the love of liberty. Tidal changes in the North and South, among Republicans and Democrats alike. Most Americans pay very little attention to public policy—we gave it up in favor of loud music and video games and barbecue and lying on the grass and looking up at the stars, the pursuit of happiness—but nonetheless we live in a social compact and expect our representatives to protect and conserve it. If they play fast and loose with it, there will come a day of reckoning.

The gaping hole in the compact is health care—42 million Americans have no health insurance and must jump through hoops in order to get treatment. I know, I used to be one of them, when I was writing fiction for *The New Yorker* and scraping along and had to take my wife twice to General Hospital in Minneapolis for treatment. Exquisite humiliation. Go to any inner-city emergency room and see suffering people filling out forms about their finances and waiting hour after hour after hour, an imperial caste system of medicine in a Christian country. National health insurance would simplify the system. The sick *will* be treated eventually—they won't be left to die in the streets—so why not do it in a humane fashion with a modicum of dignity? We've left the dark fatalistic age of medicine when the doc was a kindly old coot who held your hand as you expired. Penicillin came in and other antibiotics to fight infection and surgery took great leaps forward and now if interesting problems show up on the CAT scan we do not faint and fall over, we set out to fight the disease—and in this nation where tax-supported research propelled these great advances, our denial of the benefits to so many is downright stone-hearted. There is health care for Republican dogs and cats superior to what people get in the charity ward. Health care is a fundamental right: you go flying heedless through your youth on waxen wings, immune to illness, immortal, but then you fall to earth and need to be cared for and not lie broken on the gurney waiting for the accountants upstairs to decide if you're entitled to attention.

Mortality is the ultimate democracy. The tramp and the Trump are susceptible to the same bad news at the doctor's office, each prostate is as vulnerable as any other. You go to the Mayo Clinic in Rochester and sit in a beige waiting room among women in Armani suits, dairy farmers and assorted geezers and geezerettes of Olmsted County, pooh-bahs and nabobs chatting on cell phones, here and there an oil sheikh, and all of us praying the same continuous silent prayer: O Great Internist, let the tests come out clean and please no colonoscopy today. You imagine some pea-sized tumor in your innards that has sprouted and sent its tendrils shooting through the lymph nodes and now dense jungle growths have a grip on your vitals and in a few months people will sit in an Episcopal church and softly weep for you and plant your ashes in the ground and go have a nice lunch. We all brood over this. We are all equal in our dread of the end to this delightful life and our disbelief in our own mortality. It will be a great day in America when we finally see that everybody is cared for.

Chapter 8

AT THE CAFÉ

A liberal lady of DC
By day was tasteful and p.c.
And then after ten
She went out with men
Who were rednecks, vulgar and greasy.
"When it comes to the masculine specie,"
She said, "Believe me, I'm easy,
But liberal guys
Tend to theologize
And I'm not St. Clare of Assisi."

WHEN I AM gloomy about politics, I go sit alone in a crowded café in my neighborhood in St. Paul where the local art students like to hang out, intense young people with no clear prospects in life, and old gaffers and idlers and loafers and tourists from Iowa, genteel bohemians dreaming of the Dead and how it was to be

20 and discover Prévert and Camus. And well-fixed all-rightniks like me. I sit and inhale the smell of coffee amid the murmur of midwestern voices like water lapping on the shore. A true comfort on a cold day in April. I feel attached to this neighborhood, having lived here off and on half my life. Today, the morning paper has left me feeling stranded in a nation more like the Austro-Hungarian Empire of 1914 than the sweet land of liberty but a walk around the neighborhood can cure that. The trees are budding, lilac bushes too, girls with bare midriffs stroll past. Summit Hill was Millionaires Row, home of the Upper Fifty, an old Republican bailiwick of lumber and insurance and railroad families of the 1870s that, after a century of graceful decline, was bought up and renovated by Democrats. Liberals have a secret lust for Victoriana. I've been in plenty of these old manses with their screen porches and bay windows and turrets and piazzas and arches, attending fund-raisers for losing liberals. And some winners, including Bruce Vento, a modest hard-working guy with enormous eyebrows who represented St. Paul in Congress for twenty-four years and did good things for the homeless and for the American wilderness, fought the good fights and then came home to die of lung

cancer. And Senator Paul Wellstone, who once lived around here with his wife, Sheila. A September afternoon and fifty people standing around on a brick backyard terrace at fifty bucks a head (discounts available), a dozen bottles of $10 chardonnay and a tub of Leinenkugels, baskets of chips, chip dip, salsa, and an earnest candidate standing on the back steps, jabbing the air and talking passionately about workers' compensation, which is all over my head, and I look around and see my people, people who were milling around the St. Paul Auditorium that night in 1984 when Walter Mondale, flushed like a middleweight after a fifteen-rounder, came out to concede to Ronald Reagan. We all remember the miserable defeat of George McGovern, and the Dukakis debacle, the fall of Gore—one godawful moment after another. At present, we are in our usual disarray and widely ridiculed by angry menopausal males who equate dissent with treason, but we Democrats do not faint to hear hecklers. The only shame is to lose heart. Once again we put our money in the bucket and clap for the candidate and if anyone asked us to, we would thrust our arms in the air and spell out D-E-M-O-C-R-A-T-S and cheer. Afterward a tall guy with black hair falling over his eyes says, "Hey, Keillor!"

and it's Barry Halper, my patron saint from University days, now a big man in satellite radio, and we commiserate about turning 60 and rant about the dang Republicans, and pat each other's shoulders, and two years later meet in another backyard and hear another candidate jab the air and talk about health insurance. He is one of those wonks who use three or four acronyms per sentence and think nothing of it, which is Greek to me, but I'm a Democrat, confusion and ignorance do not discourage me.

This café is owned by locals, which we old bleeding-heart Democrats prefer to patronize, being romantic about small entrepreneurs. We would walk past a Starbucks to see if maybe there was a Stella's or a Stanley's on the next block. The little guy who mortgages his house to open the hot dog stand—that hits us where we live. My cousin used to sell vegetables out of a pickup truck at the farmers' market and grew his truck garden into a big greenhouse operation north of here, a kind and courageous and honest man, the hero of the family. Another cousin launched a software company and a third is a one-man architectural firm, designing fine churches and libraries, and another is a tire dealer, and I am a writer and the founder of *A Prairie Home Companion*, which is produced by a small independent company. Not unusual for the descendants of farmers to opt for independence.

It's a big L-shaped room with exposed brick walls and big arches, a woman-sized copy of the Statue of Liberty. The front window is steamed up; an April cold front has moved in. The coffee menu is on the wall above the cash register, *espresso, latte, cappuccino, mocha, Americano* in three sizes and all sorts of permutations, 2% or skim or whole, a variety of syrups, chocolate dust, cinnamon. Biscotti, croissants, bagels, and four flavors of muffins in a glass case. Behind the case, a girl in a white apron studies me, a marvelously attitudinous girl. Her cropped dark hair is tinged with neon blue, silver rings dangle in her eyebrows, a stud glitters in her nose, and she gives me a look of offended nobility and waits for my order. *Whatever.* She is an artist, surely. Who else would need to be so prickly? God gives to the vulnerable a great power of disdain to ward off predators. I smile at her—*I'm on your side, babes*—but she doesn't buy it. She grimaces. *Come on, Pops, pick your muffin.* I choose bran and a tall *Americano.*

A good hangout. You come in, you feel you could spend the day. The music today tends toward old blues, bottleneck guitar. Ethel Waters, Bessie Smith, Arthur Crudup. Artistly people and some writerlies and some law students slumming. Some older laptop people camp here who work at home as I do and maybe miss the office camaraderie. A gaunt beauty with chestnut hair taps away on her laptop, glancing up at the door. White jeans, purple striped stockings, yellow jersey, sunglasses parked on her head. (Not from here. LA maybe, or Minneapolis.) The laptop is the best thing for writers since the opposable thumb, a portable typewriter that doubles as a file cabinet and a spelling editor and a reference room. Students sit in twos and threes, slumped, leaning on each other, talking through their noses, and two UPS drivers on their lunch hour, and a man teaching his little tow-headed boy to play chess. Two old guys are engaged in cribbage who I guess might be between jobs right now, and coming to grips with the fact that the new job will be a big step down. One is a scrawny old dude, balding, bespectacled, beige sweater and tweed jacket and jeans, rubber shoes, maybe an old English teacher about to embark on a new career as a cashier in a parking ramp. A boy in a red T-shirt engrossed in the *Norton Anthology of English Literature* and his raven-haired girlfriend next to him, a darling such as Yeats would have been crazy about for twenty years. *I will arise, and go now, and attend the coffeeshop, And sit next to that astonishment with black hair, And the bees and the voices of Democrats like water lapping, And the purple glow of her beauty there.* She has a laptop too and I wish I could read over her shoulder and find out what someone so beautiful sounds like when she is serious. Her long dark lashes and her French mouth, her swan neck, her hair. If I were her college professor, I'd have to teach with my glasses off. She and Mr. Norton clearly are a pair and I believe this is not a good day for their romance. He goes for a refill and doesn't bother to ask if she'd like anything. When he returns, he doesn't touch her shoulder and her smile up at him is tentative. On the way home, she will turn to him and say, "I'm thinking maybe I'll go down to Chicago for a few days and visit Hillary." And he'll say, "Fine." And she'll come back from Chicago with a clearer view of things, resolved to move out of the apartment. When you've broken up a few times yourself, you can recognize the signs of breakage in others. It's interesting watching people in a café. Everybody has a story and some you'd give anything to be able to hear. Couples in love and couples falling out of love and it tugs at you as nothing on TV ever could. The old English teacher going to work at the parking ramp: *this could have happened to me*, I think, and a small voice says: *It still could, Buster*.

One thing I like about this café is the feeling, walking in here, that everyone else in the room has babysat for money, hitchhiked, had a few head-on encounters with liquor, and done hard physical labor. The summer I was 15, I picked potatoes for a month, bending down all day, filling one gunnysack after another, until I couldn't stand up straight. It's something that's useful to remember when you're older and you spend the day at a desk, and also how, after a day in the potato fields, you'd play touch football until dusk and fall into bed and be back to work at 8 A.M. ready to go. This is an experience you have in common with the others. We all climbed that mountain. No particular virtue in it, but it's a checkpoint we all passed and maybe those who skipped it lost out on the comradeship. The American Brotherhood of Potato Workers lying on the cool grass under the tree at 5 P.M., straightening their backs. I wouldn't have missed it. We all were in the same boat. We all were brought up to make something of ourselves and Don't Be a Noise on

Legs. Do Your Part. Don't Be a Crybaby. Pull Your Weight. Be a Good Worker—in Minnesota, we know what that means: it means to stick with the job though you're beat and your back aches. You rest and then you get up and go back to work. You don't let the others carry your load. This simple ethic, learned young, will help save you from becoming an empty suit. You might have some interesting peccadilloes, you might be on shaky ground theologically, but if you can keep that truck under the chute until it's loaded up with corn and drive it into town and unload at the elevator and come back for more, and do this from dawn to midnight until harvest is done, then we'll make allowances for you.

The old guys at the cribbage board grew up when I did, in the happy time before there was security. We didn't always lock our doors, and we often left the keys in the ignition, we thought nothing of lying down in a public park and taking a snooze. There were not hermetic safety seals on things. Back then people might poison a loved one but nobody would poison a perfect stranger. Now even shampoo comes with a little silver foil seal. We knew nothing of hair poisoning back in the happy time. And when you walked into the drugstore, there wasn't the miserable man in the fake police uniform and the headset standing at the door and glowering at the customers.

Back then we all thought of America as one nation where everybody ate turkey with sage stuffing for Thanksgiving and after dinner the kids went outside and played Starlight Moonlight and tore around til they were out of breath and came in and watched the Bell Telephone Hour on TV with Robert Merrill and Patrice Munsel singing Rodgers and Hammerstein and dancers making geometric shapes on the floor and then a hot rod honked and your cousin Betty came downstairs and stood in the hall and primped and spritzed some Evening in Paris behind her ears and the boy in the two-toned Chevy with the fender skirts honked again and you heard his radio playing and it wasn't the Bell Telephone Orchestra but something with a lot more drums and bass and his cigarette glowed and his hair was sculpted high on his head. He was trying out the Jimmy Dean look, but you knew his family so you didn't worry. He wasn't really bad, just young, full of piss and vinegar. You watched the show and went up to bed and left the door unlocked for Betty.

We are stoics in this room and can tolerate considerable misery without comment. Winter is long and Scandinavians can be sour and unreasonable and Minnesota drivers angry and dangerous and you can't buy wine in a grocery store or pay to see naked people here and the newspapers have gone to pot and our cities sprawl for fifty miles in all directions, and politicians are short-sighted and winter is brutal, and yet, if that's what it takes to keep out the Texans, then we're happy.

If I were cheating on my taxes or dumping green gunk in the Mississippi or willfully exposing my employees to mortal danger or drawing enormous subsidies from the public trough or if I were a Republican, I wouldn't feel at ease in this café, I'd prefer to drink my coffee in a private club with a uniformed doorkeeper lest some old crone walk over and spit in my eye. We café-goers on this cold spring day are united in a civil compact and we know it, even if we don't mention it. This compact is powerful in the Midwest, thanks to our German and Scandinavian forebears, people of the *bund*, people who looked out for each other. And when we midwesterners travel to New York or London or Paris, we wonder: if we were struck by a car and lay bleeding in the gutter, would people stop and help?—the answer, surely, is yes, but here in the Midwest, there would be no question.

One morning three years ago, I heard a shriek from upstairs, a long high-pitched primeval wail, and there was my wife on the landing, holding the stiff body of our little girl. I dashed up and took Maia in my arms and Jenny went to call 911. The child was unconscious, her breathing shallow. She went into convulsions in my arms and her body stiffened, her mouth clamped shut. I thought she was dying. Sheer silent terror on a pleasant spring morning: my four-year-old daughter dying. And in about two minutes the St. Paul fire department paramedics arrived at the door. They came in, four of them, and lifted her out of my arms. They laid her on the floor and tended to her, took her temperature (she was running a fever), put an oxygen mask on her face. One of them began explaining to me about febrile convulsions, how common they are in small children, which Jenny knew about but I didn't, and then I noticed that I was still in my underwear. I pulled on a pair of trousers and we rode off to the hospital and in short order she was okay again.

The rescue squad can get to you anywhere in St. Paul in four minutes or less. That is official policy. These folks came racing up the hill from downtown, about a mile away, but there are EMTs or paramedics at eleven of the sixteen fire stations in the city and they do about eighty runs a day. The EMTs have taken a basic course of 250 class hours, the paramedics a two-year course of more than a thousand, and they know what they're doing. They work alternate 12-hour days for a week—then take four days off, then alternate 12-hour days for another week, then six days off—for an average workweek of 56 hours. They start at $38,000 a year and after three years become journeymen and jump to $50,000. The shift starts at 8 A.M., but most of them come half an hour early to sit around and drink coffee and get ready. When you call and the dispatcher sends the alarm, the paramedics are in the truck and out the door in thirty seconds. The 911 system went into service in the Twin Cities in December 1982, paid for out of the state's general fund. But the paramedics and EMTs are St. Paul city employees. And the four-minute-or-less response represents the nature of our civil compact here in St. Paul: if you urgently need help, someone will be there before panic sets in. In the suburbs, thanks to Republicans and their code of personal responsibility, the coronary victim will have time to read the entire Gospel of St. Mark before help arrives. There is a message here: if lower taxes are your priority over human life, then we know what sort of person you are. The response to a cry for help says a lot about us as human beings. You're at a party late one night and there's a scream from out on the street, and some people stick their heads out to see if there's trouble and other people don't bother. Maybe they'd rather not know.

A few years ago, a couple who lived across the hall from us in New York came to Sunday dinner at our apartment and during dinner the husband felt dizzy and excused himself and went back across the hall where he had a stroke. His wife found him, dazed, unable to speak, a few minutes later and called me and I went over to sit with him as we waited for the ambulance. It was a long wait. Malcolm was a handsome old Scot who was quite dashing in kilts at the annual Robert Burns Night and loved their vacations on the Isle of Harris, and in his last long minutes of awareness, he lay across his bed with great dignity and looked at the door, waiting for the angel. Eventually, the paramedics arrived and bundled him over to the East Side to the hospital. By the time we arrived, forty minutes had passed. Perhaps a swifter response wouldn't have made much difference. I don't know. He died a few days later.

A Democrat knows that the leaf turns and in the human comedy we are one day spectators and the next day performers. The gains in life come slowly and the losses come on suddenly. You work for years to get your life the way you want it and buy the big house and the time share on Antigua and one afternoon you're run down by a garbage truck and lie in the intersection, dazed, bloodied, your leg unnaturally bent, and suddenly life becomes terribly challenging for six months. In the *Prairie Home* office, one summer evening a woman walked out the door to go home and was swarmed by wasps and staggered back into the building, bitten so badly that her air passage was swollen half shut. She was almost unconscious, going into shock, and collapsed in the hallway. Luckily, a colleague had stayed late at work and she called 911, and in came the St. Paul paramedics to save Deb's life. Every day at work, I see a bright capable charming woman whose memorial service I might have attended had circumstances been ever so slightly different.

Two blocks from the office lived a brilliant young professor of Middle East studies who had given birth to a little girl with Down syndrome who could not nurse and needed to be fed through a tube stuck down her nasal passage. One morning, the mother, depressed though already on antidepressants, feeling hopeless, broken-hearted at the child's misery, exhausted to the point of derangement, cut the infant's throat with a butcher knife. The mother was arrested and put in Ramsey County Jail where, a few weeks later, she managed to get a plastic garbage bag, place it over her head, tie it tight around her neck, and suffocate herself. This happened in St. Paul, Minnesota, two blocks from the office where I sit and write silly songs and Guy Noir sketches. In St. Paul, people could not get this tragedy off their minds for a long time. Long after we stopped talking about it—what more could be said?—it haunted our consciences, these two souls who had slipped through our fingers and plunged to their deaths. Somehow we could have saved them. What else, dear Lord, should we have done?

The fear of catastrophe could chill the soul but the social compact assures you that if the wasps come after you, if gruesome disease strikes down your child, if you find yourself hopelessly lost, incapable, drowning in despair, running through the rye toward the cliff, then the rest of us will catch you and tend to you and not only your friends but We the People in the form of public servants.

This is a basic necessity in a developed society. Men and women make love and have babies in the knowledge that if the baby should be born with cerebral palsy or Down syndrome or a hole in its heart and require heroic care, the people of Minnesota and of St. Paul will stand with you in your dark hour. If you are saddled with trouble too great for a person to bear, you will not be left to perish by the roadside in darkness. Without that assurance, we may as well go live in the woods and take our chances.

This is Democratic bedrock: we don't let people lie in the ditch and drive past and pretend not to see them dying. Here on the frozen tundra of Minnesota, if your neighbor's car won't start, you put on your parka and get the jumper cables out and deliver the Sacred Spark that starts their car. Everybody knows this. The logical extension of this spirit is social welfare and the myriad government programs with long dry names all very uninteresting to you until you suddenly need one and then you turn into a Democrat. A liberal is a conservative who's been through treatment.

To the hard-ass redneck Republican tax cutter of the suburbs, human misery is all a fiction, something out of novels, stories of matchstick people. He's doing fine so what's the problem? He is oblivious. George Custer knew more about the Sioux than this guy knows about the world around him. He is heavily into postponement for short-term savings and long-term disaster. He and his fellow Republicans slash the funding of social welfare programs—which has instant political appeal: ENCOURAGE RESPONSIBILITY, CUT WELFARE, SAVE $$$$$— and lo and behold, children in abusive homes can no longer be removed from those homes by social workers because there's no money to pay for alternative care, and one morning, the rednecks read in the paper about a child locked in a closet for weeks, half-starved, lying in its own feces, and they don't make the connection between their politics and the evil done to that child. The child's suffering has nothing to do with them. So the kid goes to relatives who also have a history of abuse. It's no skin off the redneck's nose. He's got a giant TV, 99 channels of cable, a snowmobile, a Hummer, a collection of guns, a boat, Jet Skis, he's sitting pretty. The demise of somebody else's kid at the hands of a drunken uncle is nothing but roadkill to him. This is the screw-you philosophy that festers under cover of modern Republicanism.

Part of the civil compact is the government that we install in office: if you and I subscribe to the compact, then I cannot tolerate a government that brutalizes you on my behalf. If suddenly on a Friday night the red lights flash and the cops yank your teenage son and his little envelope of marijuana into the legal meatgrinder and some bullet-headed prosecutor decides to flex his muscle and charge your teenager, because he had a .22 rifle in his upstairs bedroom closet, with a felony involving use of a firearm, which under our brutal sentencing code means he can be put on ice for twenty years, and the prosecutor goes at him hammer and tong and convinces a passive jury and your boy's life is sacrificed so that this creep can run for Congress next year—this is not your cross alone to bear; this violates the compact between you and me. Our war on drugs is a religious war against a pleasure-seeking minority and if your son is caught in it, like a raccoon in a bear trap, this gross injustice makes it hard for you to sit in a café with me if I turn a blind eye to what happened. If your life is blighted by rank injustice and I don't care, then you can't be happy in my company. That's why it's unpleasant to set foot in Texas. They execute human beings there with gay abandon. They railroad them through with a dimestore defense and the governor glances at the appeal and denies it and the defendant is tied to a gurney and put down like a dog. This fact leaves a sour cloud over Austin and Fort Worth and San Antonio, a grain of sand in the burrito, a lurid orange glow at the dance.

Narcissism and cruelty are twins: we expect God to cut us slack and hold others to account. And our criminal justice system easily turns sadistic: those people in handcuffs are not us. The state of Wisconsin has brought back the old chain gang and put radio-controlled stun belts on the prisoners so that a guard or trusty can flick a switch and impart a jolt of electricity that knocks a prisoner off his feet. You would not do this to anybody you knew personally, but when it comes to despised groups, we are capable of great cruelty in the name of toughness. Call a man a terrorist and you can lock him up for a long time without a trial, torture him, sodomize him, kill him if you wish. People campaign for office on their ability to be vicious to select groups of people unlikely to vote in large numbers. Teenage dope smokers, for example.

There is a basic faith here in this café: *if you work hard and pay attention and don't let the greasy tentacles of al-*

cohol or drugs wrap around you and don't take stupid shortcuts that land you in jail, you can thrive, and if catastrophe falls on you, earthquake or drought or flood or fire, the others will come to your rescue. If a wrong is done to you, it will be addressed. To right-wingers, this is the sentimental reflex of an old liberal that he got from Thomas Hart Benton murals and the songs of Woody Guthrie and old Hollywood flicks about the Little Guy, but not to me. What I feel in this café is the social contract by which people pledge comfort and support to each other in time of need, which each of us will sooner or later come to. If this contract is torn up, we'd have to buy a .357 pistol and a junkyard dog and head for the woods and stock up on dried foods. I have drawn on this contract often. My education at the U. My child has been blessed by loving teachers whose gifts were nurtured at state expense and she was rescued by the fire department. Three years ago after I suddenly turned into a wheezy old man who woke up in the night feeling suffocated, Dr. Orczulak at Mayo opened up my thorax and sewed a leaky valve in my heart, a dramatic procedure whose perfection over the past fifty years was heavily subsidized by the taxpaying public. Dr. Walt Lillehei of the University of Minnesota was a giant in the field, operating on blue babies and hopeless little kids with bad hearts—I saw pictures of them on the front page of the Minneapolis *Star* in the Fifties, smiling wanly from their hospital beds—a major news item back then: the heart of a living person stopped and opened with a knife and the bunged-up part mended as you would cobble a shoe—and despite high casualty rates and the enormous cost of each attempt, the open-heart operation was brought (thanks to public assistance) to the point of utter ordinariness, which my operation was. Everyone and his cousin has had a by-pass, or a double, or a quadruple with a one and a half gainer. No more traumatic, on the whole, than a broken leg. Thank you, America. How could I, whose life has been extended by this largesse, turn into an angry right-winger, a knee-jerk tax cutter, flogging public employees and the very idea of public service? How could a graduate of the University of Minnesota turn around after graduation and become a No New Taxes Republican and reduce his alma mater to the level of a community college? What towering ingratitude lies at the heart of the Republican Party! What a mean-spirited betrayal of the common life of this country!

ORDINARY DECENCY

A dying liberal of Berkeley
Whose mind still functioned, but murkily,
Rose up and said,
As he dropped dead,
"Will somebody please tell Studs Terkel he—"

THIS MORNING in the café, a man is telling about a
pane of glass that, I gather, fell out of a tall building
and sliced down into the street and landed fifteen feet
away from him: he has to tell somebody because this is
news, it just happened half an hour ago. Someone else saw
Sophia Loren. In northeast Minneapolis. A few years ago.
True. She was making a movie. She stood this close to me.
Someone tells about his cousin, a botanist, who got back
from Iran where twenty-five thousand people died in ten
minutes in an earthquake. The cousin loves the Iranian

people, the culture. How old is Sophia Loren? Sixty-five? She is one of the world's most stunningly beautiful women. You have to wonder about how they're constructing these office buildings nowadays if the windows are falling out.—So goes the conversation over coffee.—I couldn't live in a country where strangers don't talk freely to each other and tell stories and air their grievances and joke and gas about this and that, and George W. Bush is trying to give us that country, where taxes are cut and services are stripped and the schools go to a four-day week and the local library depends on bake sales and user fees and police and fire are outsourced to a company that provides those services and soon 10 or 20 or 30 million Americans realize they are living in the rye on the edge of the cliff. This helps cut labor costs on the plantation. The field hands line up for work and Mr. George offers them 18 cents per hour and a cold potato for lunch and they accept his generous offer. He is the boss and under him are the managers, and then there are the field hands, who live in treehouses or the backseats of cars. The bosses have their country club, and the managers have the Elks and Kiwanis and Rotary, and the field hands are allowed to sit in the public park so long as they don't spit or use bad language or play cards or speak to women. Sometimes the boss stops by and says, "Morning, Chester," and the hand looks down at the ground and says, "Morning, Mass' George" in a low tone of voice. There is an oppressive set of reticences that apply, depending on your social calculus. You stay on your side of the line. That's not America as I know it. A house divided against itself cannot stand; we cannot long endure, half predator, half prey.

If you forgot your billfold on the table of this café in St. Paul, you could come back an hour later and the girl at the counter would hand it to you, all the cash still in it. If you need a light, a smoke, directions, a quarter for the pay phone, the use of a pen, the name of a famous movie you've been trying to think of, you can get those here, no problem. That's because we know each other here. If we become a nation of strangers, this will change. On the streets of New York right after 9/11 people talked to you or talked in your vicinity and you leaned over and listened—and you heard about the cousin who stayed home from work that day, and the man with the office on the 93rd floor of the north tower who lingered over his coffee and *Times* in a diner and missed being killed that day. Republicans have no shame about exploiting 9/11 but like most catastrophes, it was democratic—the bus-boys and dishwashers in Windows on the World died along with the executives—just as war used to be. On Memorial Day, the men and women of the American Legion and VFW place little flags and flowers at the graves of veterans. There isn't a Platinum Class flag for those whose families pony up more. All soldiers are unknown in the end, death is anonymous, and the old men who troop the colors are contemptuous of the chicken hawks who never fought but enjoy speechifying about American honor to a degree that is indecent. The old men know about the terror and confusion and stink and evil of war. The most fitting memorial observance is silence. The honor guard stands, the breeze rippling the leaves, and we think our thoughts about those boys and their real sufferings and the bugler plays Taps and we turn and go home.

All those dead boys and millions of the rest of us went through the draft board physical, which once was a powerful democratic checkpoint. If you were a 17-year-old boy, you thought about the approach of your 18th birthday, it had significance. If your draft board called, you went. Even a Rockefeller had to drop trousers and spread his cheeks and bend over. Of course, the great checkpoint was military service. In the U.S. Army, my dad and his buddies learned to stand in line and accept their place in the bigger picture, and they met people utterly unlike themselves and bonded with them and thereby learned something about decency.

Back in the democratic Fifties, if I needed a ride home from Anoka, I could stand on the West River Road with my thumb out and cars would come around the bend and I'd look them straight in the windshield and think positive thoughts and smile pleasantly and most cars would whoosh past but one driver would see that my clothes were clean and my posture good and he'd stop and pick me up and I got to meet interesting people that way, people utterly unlike me, and hear some of their stories. People might say things to a kid they'd never meet again. *Let me tell you something. Don't ever get married.* Okay. *I mean it, don't get married. It's grief from morning to night.* Yes, sir. *There is nothing you can do to make them happy. Nothing.* I see. *There is nothing you can do to please them. You go the extra mile and they're mad because you're an inch short.* And you got your ride to downtown Minneapolis. This doesn't happen much anymore. It represented the trailing edge of the Thirties spirit of mutual assistance—disaster can strike anyone at any time so we do not turn people away who need something that we can provide. Downtown, in my youth, you saw little strips of paper stuck in the cracks of brick walls or telephone poles by the streetcar stops. My mother explained that they were streetcar transfers, left by people who didn't need them for people who did. No more. In Mr. Bush's America, it's screw you all the way.

America has a democratic heart. It is a generous and redemptive land where you can lift your head and know that justice and equality and a decent sympathy for the underdog are part of the music and poetry of people. We honor openness of heart, a democratic style. You are polite to the checkout girls at the Piggly Wiggly and to the shoeshine man. You do not lord it over them as if you were the grand panjandrum of Mushti and they your serfs. You don't expect people to bow in your direction. Bill Monroe, the father of bluegrass, once ran into Frank Sinatra backstage at the Grammys and said, "And what is it you do?" He honestly didn't know. Sinatra wasn't insulted. It's a big country, not some little comic-opera aristocracy, and if people don't tip their hats when you walk into the room, well, don't take it too hard. My wife was walking down upper Broadway one afternoon and saw a familiar face approach and racked her brain for the guy's name—had she played in an orchestra with him? Was he an opera singer?—and smiled at him and he smiled back at her—"How are you? Haven't seen you for a while," she said. "Fine," he said. "How are you?" "Good," she said. "You been busy?" "Yes," he said, and so it went, and as she turned away, she realized she'd been talking to the actor Robin Williams, not just another violinist.

Good manners are democratic. Your mother taught you to be kind to all whom you meet, everyone matters, don't look down your nose at the sales clerk, don't jerk the cleaning lady around. When I run into Minnesotans in foreign places, I notice their good manners, which aren't about forks or the intricacies of protocol but about kindness and the ability to see beyond yourself. They don't bitch about the weather or the service or the food or the foreignness, they look on the bright side.

Your mother didn't raise you to be a jerk who sucks up to power and treats the help like dirt. Go ahead and prosper, but mind your manners. And don't pick on the vulnerable. You go backstage after the Lake Wobegon High School production of *My Fair Lady* in which your niece played Eliza like a fence post all night and there she is, trembling, shaken, ashen-faced, and you say, "It was good, Lindsey. You really connected with that audience, it had so much resonance and honesty." So she doesn't torture herself over this debacle. So she has no talent—so what? No need to face the whole truth all at once.

Sports is a democratic world: everyone sees the ball game for himself and snaps his own mental picture of the runner sliding home, safe or out, and your outrage at the ump for a lousy call is genuine. The corporate sky box is the worst place to sit; you miss the camaraderie of the bleachers and the acerbic wit of young men drinking beer. A player earning $14 million a year doesn't bother us at all. He didn't land the job because he's the owner's nephew, he got it because he could cover the shortstop position and hit the curve ball, and it's baseball that we pay to go see so why shouldn't talent be rewarded? But if he bobbles an easy grounder or takes a called third strike down the middle of the plate, the bleachers will have plenty to say to him.

I sit in the ballpark and think of young men on the troopships sailing the Atlantic to North Africa and Sicily and Normandy, afraid of death and yet believing in their own survival. They planned to escape death and return home to live the life that we live now, loose and easy, watching the ball game on a June night, eating a bratwurst slathered with mustard. Right up to the moment of their death, they dreamed of this good life, the outfielders poised in the twilight, the little kids tearing around under the stands, the pitcher peering in at the catcher and going into his stretch, checking the runner at first—a pure democracy: all batters get three strikes, the strike zone the same for everyone, also the base paths and fences.

When the old white CEO gets in a cab at the airport, if he wants to converse with the young black cabdriver, sports is what they can talk about. Not their summer vacation plans, not cars, not homes, not politics. Basketball.

Then there is the democracy of jokes. Telling a joke right is a skill, like hammering a nail, and anyone can learn it. *The man walks into the bar with a handful of dog turds and says to the bartender, "Hey, look what I almost stepped in!"* Anybody can tell that joke. You join a group of strangers in a bar and listen to their jokes and after an appropriate length of time, you tell yours. *The reason men fart more than women is that women don't keep their mouths shut long enough for the pressure to build up.* You tell a simple joke simply. You deliver it dry, not too much topspin, and you do the setup in a clear concise manner—*a guy takes his boy deer hunting and they're creeping through the woods*—and here you can embroider a little, and then you feed them the punch line—*and the man says "Son, this is your first deer hunt, it's a very important time in your life, it marks your passage into manhood, do you have any questions?" and the boy says, "Yes. If you die of a heart attack, how do I get home?"* If you tell it well and don't oversell the joke, or apologize, or laugh more than they do, and if the joke is a new one, you'll be welcome here. *A man went to the Lutheran church on Sunday morning and after the service he stopped to shake the pastor's hand. He said, "Preacher, I'll tell you, that was a helluva sermon. Damned fine." The pastor said, "Thank you, sir, but I'd rather you didn't use that sort of language." The man said, "I was so damn impressed with that sermon I dropped a check for ten thousand dollars in the collection plate." The pastor said, "Holy shit."*

Chapter 10

A CIVILIZED PEOPLE

There was an old liberal named Kurt
Who wore his heart on his shirt.
The poor pay of teachers
Or the death of small creatures
Left him shaken and visibly hurt.

THE BLUE-TINGED girl brings my coffee with a grand hauteur that makes me sort of proud of her. It's that old piss-on-your-shoe spirit of the underdog class that seems rather scarce these days. Corporate America is very successful at training this out of people through flattery ("You are a vital member of the HellMart family") and terror ("Smile and show your gums or you'll be fired and have to leave town to find work"). School tries to knock it out of you, the church coaxes you to be passive and sweet, but the human spirit is resilient and

153

the blue-tinged girl refuses to curtsy. "Coffee smells good," I say. A faint smile or grimace on her lips. "Better than Starbucks," I say. "Right," she says. My irony detector detects irony. She reminds me of myself when I started to think that I was a writer. There wasn't much evidence of it, so what could I do but try to look the part, smoke unfiltered smokes, practice irony, and carry myself with some grandeur. Here she is, making maybe eight bucks an hour with tips, not beautiful or especially gifted or smart, but with a grand attitude and a big urge to be somebody. I wish her well. I wish I could give her a word of advice: *lighten up, kid.*

"You want lunch?" she says. The lunch menu is written on a blackboard on the wall. Then I notice the green Wellstone pin on her shirt. "Did you know Paul?" I say. She nods. I imagine he came in here to eat and, being Paul, he reached over the counter and shook everybody's hand. I don't: I'm a writer. We are lurkers in corners, observers, and fishers among men. Paul relished public life on the highways and byways, bobbing into a crowded café, encountering people. When he went out for lunch, he made a point of sticking his head in the kitchen afterward and shaking hands with the cooks and the dishwashers. I was a dishwasher once and if a U.S. Senator had appeared in the steam of the scullery and taken my hand, it would've made my day, that's for sure. You saw Paul in the Twin Cities airport, waiting to fly back to Washington, talking, a little knot of passersby around him, bouncing on the balls of his feet as he talked. He wasn't seduced by comfort and flattery and he kept his point of view as an outsider. He served in the Senate for twelve years, a short voluble Jew representing a state of tall laconic Scandinavians and Germans. People liked him who didn't necessarily share his opinions, because he was loyal to his people, the bus drivers, the waitresses, the dishwashers, the cleaning ladies. He wasn't a Senator for rent, he spoke up for people who need speaking up for, he saw things from ground level, like a novelist, like a Democrat. He and Sheila had an apartment three blocks from here. On the morning of October 25, 2002, they drove down Selby Avenue to the downtown St. Paul airport to board the charter plane that would crash in the cold fog in the woods. That was a year and a half ago and the blue-tinged girl is still loyal to him. Electioneering is a demanding discipline, a combination of marathon dancing, flagpole sitting, and competitive pie eating. He'd done that for a year and was a month away from beating his slippery opponent and getting to take a vacation with Sheila and spend time at the movies, and his pilots got off the beam and landed in the trees. He was afraid of flying and not much else. He preached against fear, as people of my generation should. We old Democrats think of them often: Paul and Sheila and daughter Marcia and their staff, Will and Mary and Tom, dying a few days before Election Day, 2002.

Our beloved land has been fogged with fear—fear, the greatest political strategy ever. Easy to plant: an ominous silence, distant sirens, mouth breathing. A drumbeat of whispered warnings and alarms to keep the public uneasy and silence the opposition. And in a time of vague fear, you can appoint bullet-brained judges, strip the bark off the Constitution, eviscerate the federal regulatory agencies, bring public education to a standstill, stupefy the press, lavish gorgeous tax breaks on the rich, and your approval numbers will stay high.

Meanwhile, Republicans do very little for their own people—look at the family farm in the Midwest: a sinking ship. That courageous and intelligent tribe is walking the Trail of Tears. The number of dairy farms is in steep decline, even as milk production rises, thanks to factory farms with herds of 500 hormonally souped-up cows who put down 20,000 pounds of milk a year. Dairy farming was what permitted very industrious people to earn a living on poor land, it's fundamental to our culture, and we're sad and pained to see it go. The Republican prairie towns are drying up and blowing away, the supermarket bulletin boards post notices that say ALCOHOLISM and DOMESTIC ABUSE and SUICIDE with hotlines to call for confidential help. Meanwhile the urban tribes of bullshitters are prospering, holding their bullshit powwows in big hotel ballrooms, bloviating about Strategizing the Global Deconstruct, monkey talk, but the b.s. industry is vertically structured, so if No. 1 and No. 2 and No. 3 take something seriously, then you (No. 11) take it *very* seriously. Farmers are horizontal, especially in North Dakota, and must actually know how to do real things. Manure will go only so far for them. The fence lines have been plowed through and the fields have become a half mile long and there's no such thing as the lower forty anymore, it's the lower four hundred. There are a few farms where you still see thirty or forty Holsteins standing out in the mud and manure, but the thousand-head dairy factory is becoming the norm. People who don't have that kind of capital try to scratch together a living making crafts or trading stocks on the Internet or dealing antiques, which there are a lot of in the country. They scrape along, meanwhile braggarts and bullies rise to power and acclaim. *Why, Lord?* And why does the Minnesota State Legislature make it legal for anybody with a Wheaties box top to carry concealed weapons so that now Your Houses of Worship must display an ugly sign, GUNS ARE NOT PERMITTED ON THESE PREMISES? Why this Wild West weirdness in our midst? It rankles us, and so does our Republican governor plumping for the death penalty (no executions here since the hanging of William Williams in 1906 when the trap was sprung and the man fell and his feet touched the floor and three deputies had to grab hold of the rope and haul him up and hang on for fifteen minutes while he slowly strangled—the grisliness of it civilized us for a hundred years) in the wake of public anguish after the kidnapping and murder of a lovely young woman in the Red River Valley last November, her tragic death to be the door to barbarism. The rancid vapors of right-wing radio swirl around us and the spirit of the prosecutor stalks the land. The war in Iraq is bad business, the administration's foreign policy is for domestic consumption, security is mostly for show—elderly ladies are asked to remove their shoes while cargo containers drift over the border uninspected. The government is in the hands of blackjack dealers. But have courage. All is not lost. This is not Iran, or the Age of the Hapsburgs, it's America. The people will be pushed just so far. They will clap for the naked president just so long and then they'll laugh and when they start laughing they won't stop.

Meanwhile, I'll have an egg salad sandwich. Cheap at the price: $3.85. I give her a ten and get change and put a five in her tip jar and she sees this. She doesn't smile— she can't be bought—but her eyes soften. Overtipping is allowed. She spreads mayo on the bread and a half cup of egg salad and two leaves of lettuce and slices it on the diagonal and sets it on a plate.

I take a seat at a corner table facing the window. A blustery spring day. The mutter of cars and buses as they pull up to the STOP sign. Western Avenue, once the city limit back when little farms lay between St. Paul and the milling city of Minneapolis. On the corner is the old drugstore where F. Scott Fitzgerald came to buy his cigarettes the summer of 1919 when he was living in his parents' garret, a Princeton dropout and failed ad man and former lieutenant who never got to fight, and wrote the novel that made him famous, *This Side of Paradise*. Book and author caught the crest of the Jazz Age and swept to fame, romance, celebrity, wealth, happiness, insanity, desperation, failure, desperate resolution, vain hope, sudden death, but when he walked down that sidewalk over there and turned the corner at Selby Avenue he was just a writer engrossed in the task of trying to turn a loser into a winner. He was born two blocks from here in 1896. His mother had lost two babies and he was the third, and she devoted herself to him and from her lavish love sprouted a boy who believed he could throw the long touchdown pass and win the unattainable girl, be a war hero, and write the Great American Novel.

St. Paul was an outpost to him, a city of Swedes and onionheads, a cold colony he would escape and find his way to Manhattan, and Paris and Hollywood. The land of bitter winds and smug self-effacing people. And yet when Fitzgerald said, "My generation of radicals and breakers-down never found anything to take the place of the old virtues of work and courage and the old graces of courtesy and politeness," he was talking about St. Paul.

When I was still in high school, I came over to this neighborhood to walk around and think about him. It astonished me to read the opening of *Gatsby* and "Winter Dreams" and *The Crack-Up* and think, "The man who wrote this grew up a few blocks from Jean and Les's house." When Grandpa rode the streetcar to St. Paul to take out his naturalization papers, the pretty boy in knee pants and swinging his book strap might have been Fitzgerald. Up and down the avenues, past the old brick and stone mansions of the Hills and Griggses and Weyerhausers and Ordways, I anguished in a rather grand way about death, my death, and how nobody ever would know I had the grand ambitions that I had, poor little me, dying unknown, unsung, the tiny obituary *(Student Succumbs to Flu)*. I used to sit on a little triangle of grass behind a statue of Nathan Hale, his hands tied behind his back, about to be hanged, and watch approaching headlights on Summit Avenue and think, in a satisfying and literary way, about how alone and lost and misunderstood I was. (In fact, was not; was encouraged by many, and found good teachers wherever I looked; had been lucky my whole life.) I looked at a graceful old house and imagined how happy life would be if only I owned it, a brick palazzo with French doors opening onto a terrace from which I could extrapolate a life of affection and amiable conversation. Dark ladies smoking Herbert Tareytons, their long legs draped over a stone balustrade, speaking in low urgent tones about a book, an important book, terribly important, *the* book, and they rise as they talk, and their expressive hands map out the New World this book foresees in the mist, having torn the roof off the old one. I love the conversation of passionate believers. I was brought up by cautious people who taught me to make haste slowly and yet I have always wanted to get more than one life including some passionate ones, a St. Paul one but also a Parisian one, and a cowboy life, of course, and a show-biz one, and a literary one, and a secret life as, say, a bartender in a seaside town in northern California. I lived a lot of lives vicariously as a reader and then invented a few lives of my own. When, at the age of forty, I bought a big green frame house with a porch on Goodrich Avenue, it only made me more restless. I pulled up stakes and moved five blocks away to a brick house with a walled garden, then jumped to a belle epoque apartment in Copenhagen where I paced and plotted my escape, then to Central Park West in New York, then to a log cabin in a grove of aspens in Wisconsin with a family of wild turkeys who came and went. And then landed back here in St. Paul, near Nathan Hale, and here I have stopped.

A couple of patrons nod to me as I walk by and I nod back. I hear my name whispered, and the sound of it triggers a reflex: *you're being watched, try to look intelligent.* I am in that gray eminence stage of life when people take you for someone notable though they don't know what for. "Are you famous?" a girl asked me once; I shook my head. A person doesn't have to be if he doesn't want to. Fame makes you moody and the writing goes dead and you grab hold of the gin bottle. So don't get famous. Line up with the rank and file where the fun is.

Sometimes I feel a hot stare and detect hostility—we Minnesotans don't care to be patronized, as the old *Variety* headline said, STIX NIX HIX PIX, and plenty of Minnesotans are crusty about me and Lake Wobegon, thinking I've hixed them. Nonetheless I am perfectly content here.

When my mother was 15, she lived a few blocks from here with Aunt Jean and Uncle Les. She'd been sent over from Minneapolis by her dad because she had a rebellious streak, went to movies, liked to talk with boys, went to dances. She attended St. Paul Central and studied to be a nurse and after school she went around selling homemade cookies to help pay her way in the world. I think of her, carrying a boxful of bags of cookies along Summit Avenue and screwing up her courage to march to the door and ring the bell. And the lady opens the door and Mother says, "Good afternoon, would you care to purchase a dozen fresh peanut butter cookies?" And a balloon appears over the lady's head: *NO*. And a string of bubbles and another balloon: *There ought to be a law against beggars*. And the door is closed, *whammmm*, and the girl blushes and her heart sinks and she heads toward the next house. A long afternoon on the cookie route.

It's like the beginning of a fairy tale, "The Peanut Butter Cookie Girl," in which she is about to eat all her cookies and perish in a snowbank and then a prince shows up with a crystal slipper in hand. The truth is, my mother would've found a prince like Fitzgerald insufferable. She had the plain good manners of working people who didn't indulge flamboyant self-dramatization. My mother can be very sniffy toward rich people and so could Dad. He felt superior to people who spent money to show off. Felt uneasy in fancy houses or around wealthy people. Had no desire to meet the Queen. Preferred a Ramada Inn to the Ritz. No Cadillac, thank you. He took pride in modesty and spending money carefully because, after all, you worked hard for it, didn't you?

My 16 oz. *Americano* with an extra shot of espresso, two biscotti, comes to $4.95. I am 61 and in my mind the value of a cup of coffee has stayed right around 35 cents but I'm willing to pay extra for the pleasure of being with Democrats. I grew up with these people, they are where my world begins. A civilized people, who love the hubbub of the city, the yawp and jabber of the crowd, the slang and gossip, the old songs and legends, the great bootstrap stories. The ambitious immigrant who puts his kids through college. The person who overcomes a handicap to climb the mountain. The lucky lunch ladies who for fourteen years put a quarter apiece in the pot every payday to buy a lottery ticket and then won, Phyllis, Susan, Judith, Roseanne, Betty, Mary, Alice, Donna, Barbara, Karen, Doreen, Cathy, Elaine, Nancy, and two Kathleens, $95 million, and the next morning went to work and served lunch. The people who persevere. Duke Ellington and his elegant band barnstorming the segregated South, adored in London and Paris and Copenhagen and they couldn't get a cup of coffee in Georgia or Alabama. The young painters in their low-rent lofts in the Village when New York was the center of the art world. The poets who slept in train stations and sold their blood as they gathered their gift together. Dancers subsisting on ramen noodles, actors who walked ten miles to save bus fare, violinists scarfing up leftovers at the country club wedding reception, their big meal of the week, novelists scraping by without health insurance, writing until 3 A.M. month after month with no idea that anything will come of this rigorous life. There's a reason why 95% of people in the arts are Democrats. An artistic gift is dropped on you by God and if you attend to the gift and are true to it, you will sometimes be in serious need of a helping hand. Art is an imperative stronger than commerce. Republicans don't understand this. They cherish you if you're rich and famous, they can't do enough for you if there's nothing you need, but when you're hard up, don't go to the front door of the Manor, go around to the back and the hired help will take you in. And art speaks for the powerless. A poor child in the street is a better choice for point of view than the tycoon in his study: this we know. Ishmael rather than Ahab; Huck rather than Judge Thatcher. The democracy of letters is hospitable to outsiders: readers are curious and adventuresome and want to see beyond their own bailiwick and crave news from the wrong side of town. Artists tend toward an outsider point of view, are drawn toward stories of failure, know that satire is always in behalf of the underdog and the outnumbered, and are committed to the forbidden and dangerous and thrilling thing, namely, the truth. This makes them unwelcome in the Republican Church, which is not (thank you very much) about the outsiders, the wrong side of town, or poor children.

Chapter 11

THE GOOD DEMOCRAT

A young social worker named Dede
Came home from work and said, "Sweetie,
I feel sort of wobbly
So pour me a Chablis
And don't be emotionally needy."

1. Democrats distrust privilege and power. Power unchecked runs amok, tears up the garden, and the privileged become sluggish and dull if nobody talks back to them. We think royalty should ride bicycles and carry their own luggage; we think famous people ought to fix their kids' breakfasts and attend their school concerts. We don't like divas who abuse the help, or rock stars who devastate hotel rooms, or CEOs who get big raises when the ship is sinking, or anybody riding high who spits on the peons below. If you earn $14 million a year, you better keep your nose clean and not try to write off your family vacation as a business expense. (Congressman Martin Olav Sabo of Minneapolis authored the Income Equity Act that would deny companies a tax deduction for excessive executive compensation, that is, the portion of the CEO's salary that is more than 25 times the salary of the lowest-paid full-time company employee. If starting pay for the lowliest file clerk is $18,000, then the CEO's salary in excess of $450,000 is not deductible as a business expense. The act has been kept bottled up in the House Ways and Means Committee, a little nod toward democracy that is anathema to Republicans.)

I suppose the most powerful man is a deranged person with a loaded gun who has nothing to lose, and here are we, vulnerable because we have loved ones and a life that is precious to us, and between him and us stands the power of government. I choose not to walk through the streets of St. Paul with a pistol in my pocket because it strikes me as slightly demented. Because it's not 1845. Because having one doesn't fascinate me. Because my sympathy is with the cops who have to think about guns every time they walk up to a front door or pull someone over to the side of the road. I count on the civil society to defend me. Defending the powerless against the powerful is a basic task of government, an article of faith in the America that I grew up in. Walking into the supermarket, you are powerless to investigate the meatpacker who packaged these Glo-Brite wieners so the government must do it for you. The government is there to do battle with those who would sell you cars that are firebombs or TV sets that cause cancer in small children or vitamins that make hair sprout on your palms or hamburgers made from deceased springer spaniels. Every year the bank examiners come around to look at the books and make sure that the president of First Texas Trust isn't siphoning your money to his account in Geneva—how did Republicans manage to make this an issue? *You can't suddenly change the rules to suit yourself. You can't stop the train and kick off the people you don't like. You can't tower over people and roar and screech and spray saliva on them. You can't prey on the preoccupied and slip in a 2% surcharge on the electric bill and thereby filch a billion dollars a few cents at a time. You can't sell bad meat or water the beer or charge 25% interest or piss in the public water supply. You can't put a quarter in the collection plate and take a dollar out.* Democrats thought that this was understood.

2. *Equality is Democratic bedrock.* Democrats believe in writing your own story and putting it up against other people's on a level court and let the game begin and more power to you, sing your song and do your dance, but don't be under the illusion that you invented yourself. Don't be so superior you're offended at the thought of the progressive income tax. There is an old geezer in a captain's cap with a hundred buttons pinned to it and an electric fan suspended from the brim, an orange vest with badges and flag decals, who rides around the neighborhood from time to time on a three-wheeler with a fringed green canopy over it and a Bush-Cheney bumper sticker and a horn and a bell, with a look of royalty and privilege about him as if he were the Duke of Northumberland accompanied by the Royal Fusiliers, which is fine by me—self-expression is a fine thing—but I look at him and realize why I love the liturgy of the Anglican Church: because we didn't write it, those are everybody's words. Collective expression is the rare thing; self-expression is common as dandelions. An old Democrat is of course in favor of freedom of self-expression—go tattoo whatever vulgarity you want on your forehead, go sound your barbaric war cry—but this old Democrat prefers the King

James and the Lord's Prayer and the old Lutheran table grace (*Be present at our table, Lord. Be here and everywhere adored. Thy children bless and grant that we may feast in paradise with Thee*) and all the common treasures from blues to children's rhymes to John Henry and Frankie and Johnny and Jon Jonson of Wisconsin to knock-knock and lightbulb jokes to aphorisms that express the ordinary skepticism of people. We reside in a city of memory and share the avenues with the others. It is a wicked world, in which the power to do harm is so great and the power to do good so slight and an angry fool can do more damage in a day than a hundred wise men can fix in a year, but here we are, we must do our best and do it as a people and when I'm in a crowd singing "America the Beautiful" I get emotional about the pilgrims' feet and the alabaster cities and the heroes proved in liberating strife, which belong to us all and don't need improvement.

A writer starts out trying to express himself and show how thoughtful he is and even occasionally brilliant and as he loses interest in that, what sustains him is the love of the common language, English, whose beauty is that it has been enriched from below, by street patois and criminal lingo and teen slang and black English and immigrant languages. Prizes for brilliance are a dime a dozen: what's really special is to write something that speaks for others.

3. *We Democrats are inclusive and integrationist to the core.* We cross social lines and climb through strata. We are fond of cities where people merge and life bubbles up from below, where high society hangs out with show folks, bankers meet dancers, Lutherans consort with Catholics, Samaritans mill among Judeans and black and pink and brown and Jesus moves among the publicans. If we go to Copenhagen, we choose not to stay at the luxury hotel where the staff is careful never to speak Danish in your presence, we prefer to stay with a Danish family so we can eat what they eat for breakfast, watch their TV shows, meet their kids, feel that we've brushed elbows with real life. We think gated communities are creepy, exclusiveness on principle is un-American. The all-male golf club is a charming relic of Victorian times, something out of P. G. Wodehouse, and God bless the old boys in their knickers with their mashies and niblicks, but

leave me out, please. Every time I've found myself in exclusive surroundings—sitting on the dais at a dinner, mingling with the thousand-dollar donors—I feel a sad diminution of energy and spark. Irreverence is the engine of wit and you're more likely to find it in the cheap seats. I'd rather not travel to places like the Middle East or Indonesia where an American travels from one secure compound to another: I'd rather stay home and be a free man than a prisoner of security. The Ritz is the Ritz, a fortress against happenstance, but a person craves street life and a day spent bumping around in Brooklyn or Montmartre or Marylebone Street. Whitman said, "I find letters from God dropped in the street and every one is signed by God's name." God's grace is in the street, among the tourists and the hayshakers. I walk along Wabasha Avenue in St. Paul and a man steps up and asks, "Aren't you Garrison Keillor?" I am, and he sticks out his hand and says, "I've never read your books but I've heard a lot about you." And pauses a beat and says, "You don't suppose you could spare a few bucks for an old bum on the street?" What excellent timing the man has. He grins at me and touches my arm. He could be a fundraiser for Yale or the Metropolitan Opera, but instead he shares his talent with the general public. So I reach in my pocket and find a bill and it's a twenty, more than I was planning to donate, but I hand it to him, and why not. Genius should be rewarded.

4. Democrats are city people at heart, even if we love the country and small town life, as I do, nonetheless the city is the crowning achievement of society. A farm is a farm but a city is history. The Lord makes counties but cities are built on the love of conversation and the profound industriousness in our natures, the need to be busy reshaping the world, peddling our wares, making coffee, jabbering, ordering new stationery. We St. Paul Democrats cherish old buildings and the history of our steamboat and railroad town, and the stories of James J. Hill and Archbishop Ireland, the French who settled in Frogtown, the Swedes of Swede Hollow, the shanty Irish, the Mexicans on the West Side. And so we fight against the 16-lane freeways the Republicans want to build to usher themselves swiftly and smoothly from their office towers to their distant green paradise. We scrap for neighborhood development money and fight for the branch library, the little park down the street, the cul-de-sac to defeat the speeders.

We are pedestrians. Walking is a cure for the blues and it's the way to look at stuff. St. Paul is a walking city, like New York or San Francisco. You amble down Selby Avenue and check the health of the boulevard trees and listen to the birds tweedling in them, see the brown beer bottles under the hedge, the dog delicately pissing on the tree, see the bees hovering around yellow petals—good news that perhaps we haven't yet poisoned the garden—and you amble farther, your disposition sweetened by a little exertion, you pick up the common parlance and the hum and rattle of the street and other pedestrians, the different shades of faces, odd signature bits of clothing, mannerisms, interesting gaits, manifest attitudes, dramatis personae, snatches of dialogue drifting past, phrases of love and irritation, slang, vagrant obscenities. Benevolent children and their dogs, coffee and pizza smells in the air, boom boxes, the whine of tires, the rumble of buses with enormous portraits of news anchors on the sides all air-brushed and dopey like news anchors in every American city and in the bus windows above their vacant mugs are the Edward Hopper bus riders heading downtown to clean the offices, peddle papers, wash dishes, a busload of long-suffering humanity. And the lovers, faces shining, out for a walk, newly joined, oblivious.

I like to hang out in New York, on the Upper West Side, a sort of National Left-Wing Park and Bird Sanctuary, and walk up Broadway past the street where George Gershwin wrote "Rhapsody in Blue" and the building Isaac Bashevis Singer lived in when he wrote his tales of Jewish village life in Europe—Holden Caulfield's hotel is nearby where he met the prostitute—and feel in the soles of my feet the vital connection between liberals and cities and artists: the common faith that genius and courage and artistic energy rise up from below and if a nation puts too great burdens on the young and the poor and the dispossessed, if the strata harden, the nation will stifle its own genius. You don't encourage invention and ambition by giving a quarter-million-dollar tax break to a $15-million-a-year man. Give the bus driver's bright children a chance to get a great education for free. That's an investment. Board the New York subway in the morning among the young editorial assistants and fledgling security traders; ride in the early evening with violinists and cellists heading for work at Lincoln Center and in the Broadway pits. Walk into the deli and there's Emanuel Ax, one of the greatest pianists on the planet, looking over the cheese selection. Not far away is the neighborhood of Langston Hughes, Allen Ginsberg, Fats Waller, Billie Holiday, Thelonious Monk, and Edward Kennedy ("Duke") Ellington, who all came bubbling up from the ranks, and Ellington's great arranger/composer Billy Strayhorn ("Take the 'A' Train," "Lush Life," "After All") who was gay before that was permissible in broad daylight. So many artists flocked to the city of New York because it has always been okay to be gay there. In the 1850s, Walt Whitman traveled freely in the bohemian gay demimonde and behaved flamboyantly for his time and nobody tried to run him out of town, the same Whitman whose "O Captain, My Captain" was one of my dad's favorite poems. It's a liberal city and it relishes people who are exercising their freedom and having a big time.

It's okay to be an artist or a writer in New York, same as it's okay to be alone. You can eat alone in a café and not feel weird, or the corner deli will sell you half a sandwich and one small brownie. It's okay to talk to yourself in public. Okay to go around on Rollerblades wearing a Donald Duck mask. It's okay to cry in public. No one will think less of you, and people may even offer you some of their medication, or tell you about something going on in their lives that's worse. Same deal in the Democratic Party. Be yourself. Had George W. Bush been a Democrat, he wouldn't have had to deny his colorful past. Cocaine? Tell us about it. Draft-dodging? We know about that too. Among Republicans I feel like a rare osprey, stuffed, labeled AUTHOR. Among Democrats I'm not all that different from anybody else.

5. *Democrats believe in individualism.* Social class does not tell the story, nor religion or political party or race or nationality. The important distinctions are between individuals, not between groups. Between two siblings, a vast unbridgeable gulf might exist, whereas between male and female, white and black, straight and gay, Eastern and Western, rich and poor, Democrat and Republican, there is ever the possibility of liaison, friendship, union, miraculous intimacy. People who ought to be enemies are not necessarily. You and I, whoever we are, drifting down the Mississippi on a raft under the stars, fugitives

from repression and intolerance, make common cause even though I am Christian and you are something else—this is the spirit I've always found among rank and file Democrats. So-called identity politics is Pundit Speak and nothing important to real Democrats. We believe that individuals are mysterious and elude attempts to categorize them, that all true stories are about individuals and stories purporting to represent Womanhood, Manhood, Jewishness, the African American Experience, Gayness, the South, the Rural Midwest, are fairy tales, sermons, promotional copy. The Great American Story is Huck Finn sticking with the nigger Jim and not betraying him to authorities. The westward migration was away from the class-bound money-dominated East toward the frontier where a friendlier spirit of individualism prevailed and a man was not held in contempt because he was broke or drunk or dressed oddly. (Oscar Wilde was a big hit when he toured the mining camps of the West.) The legends of the Great Depression and Dust Bowl and the Good War are about perseverance but also about grace and generosity between individuals who didn't know each other. The friendship of the prince and the pauper. Unlikely friendship is a pure American theme. The strangers in the club car on the Sunset Limited, in the Chatterbox Café on Main Street, and now on the Internet, the great urge to be understood as individuals, not types. In Europe we are thought naive for our rush to be friends and exchange phone numbers and make lunch dates. To a Dane, friendship is no simple matter, but an American leans toward you and starts talking about his childhood, his family, and may tell about his bipolar problem or his AA experience or his sufferings at the hands of his children, and it spurs him on if you are Danish, he insists on trying to leap that gap. The reason for fairness as a political principle is simple—you don't screw people who are, or could be, might soon be, your friends.

6. Democrats are union guys. The spiritual base of the party is the union, that grand Victorian institution that proposes that employees have a say in the workplace and bargain as a group and not be beaten down one by one. The holy martyrs who opened the way to labor unions were those Jewish immigrant women, some of them teenagers, locked by their bosses into the Triangle Shirtwaist Factory in Greenwich Village on March 25, 1911, who, when the fire broke out in the scrap bins, had no escape and leaped to their deaths, 146 of them. Now Wal-Mart is locking its employees into the warehouses at night to discourage pilfering, so not much has changed. At United Parcel Service, the starting wage for drivers is $8.70 an hour, about what it was thirty years ago, believe it or not. Unions are a good idea unless you are planning to win the lottery. They fight for the skilled jobs that pay $25 an hour or more, enough to enable you to buy a house and have children.

In my line of work, I encounter the American Federation of Musicians, which, among many other things, enforces a few basic work rules so that management (me) can't work musicians overtime without paying overtime. At least, that's the idea. In fact, musicians are as scared as UPS drivers of getting sacked, scared to speak up, to be troublemakers. Classical musicians are in oversupply—three hundred violists might rush to fill one vacancy—and orchestra strikes are rare. These are the people, beautifully trained, neurotic perfectionists, who perform for the carriage trade at the opera and the ballet, who do *Messiah* and *The Nutcracker*, who transport you with the Beethoven *Pastoral Symphony* and break your heart with the Mahler Fourth, and in the end they are *workers*, who worry about pensions and health benefits. Even if you can play that gorgeous French horn solo in Mendelssohn's *A Midsummer Night's Dream*, you still need to pay your kids' dentist.

I met my hero S. J. Perelman once at a dinner and sat across the table from him, stunned with admiration, trying to frame a compliment that would be substantial but not grandiose, and then he leaned over and groused about *The New Yorker* and its miserly treatment of writers, asked me how much they were paying me, shook his head when I told him, said I was worth more than that, said it was a battle he'd been fighting all his life, this assumption on the part of management that we were all goddamned Du Ponts, and this brotherly conversation, like a couple of metalworkers grousing over lunch, endeared him to me forever. To be regarded as a fellow worker by S. J. Perelman meant more to me than just about any prize.

Unions are a little fence against sadism. You can't, even if you're a genius with wild hair and a long baton, keep the orchestra rehearsing through their scheduled break. Even if you're tuned to the universal harmony of the spheres, people still have the right to pee. Even if you come to the end of rehearsal and *only need five more minutes*, you can't have them without paying for fifteen or thirty, whatever the contract says. So geniuses learn to watch the clock and plan their time. The union is a conservative force, resists change, is wary of innovation, and that can be maddening (though the same can be said of the National Association of Broadcasters, or the American Medical Association, both of them on the trailing edge of progress), but the union seeks to protect the dignity of its people, and that is its nobility. Without the union, they'd be treated like Holsteins; with it, they can moo at you and if you want to fire them, you have to follow procedure. You can't just shoot them in the knees.

7. A Democrat begins with sympathy for the helpless, especially children and the elderly. Sympathy is the barometer of our humanity; to the extent that we share each other's griefs and joys, we are fully alive. A person so trapped in his own head and obsessed with his own minutiae that news of earthquakes, hurricanes, drought, genocide, terror, ships sinking, trains derailing has little meaning to him, is cut off, a man without a species. He reads the story about the family who burned up in their shack, from the explosion of a kerosene stove, but it happened three miles away, no concern of his. He hears a child shriek outside but he has no children so he doesn't go to the window. From here, it is not far to the villagers going about their business downwind from the ovens of Auschwitz. We Democrats are not nannies and our interest in, say, putting helmets on bikers or making people use inclusive pronouns is vastly less than in saving innocent children from lead poisoning, the half-million toddlers in poor neighborhoods who ingest paint chips and dust and suffer brain damage, thanks to the carelessness of adults. You see welfare parents with their children and sometimes you want to grab the parents and shake them, they are so clueless and foul-mouthed and cruel, but you can't, so you hope that the social workers in Child Protection have enough funding to keep up with their caseload.

Sympathy is a basic creaturely trait, the vibration of one's being at the cry of another human—the old lady with swollen feet who clambers aboard the jam-packed bus, the woman struggling toward the gate at the airport holding one infant and pushing another in a stroller and hauling two carry-on bags, the old man climbing over the icy snow bank on the corner, the abused child, the wounded hero languishing in red tape, the old doo-wop singer cheated by the big recording label, the man on death row unfairly accused and railroaded through— your heart goes *twang*, and you offer a hand. If you don't, then I will; if neither of us does, then someone will. This is the measure of a decent community, we refuse to watch suffering and turn away.

I grew up reading *Black Beauty* and *Heidi* and *Hans Brinker, or the Silver Skates* and other books about abused underdogs redeemed in the end, which excited my pity, a strong emotion in a child. When the good horse was mercilessly beaten, I wept and could hardly read more. Now, if I sit passively and let the old lady stand clinging to a strap and don't offer my seat as the bus pulls away, I am deeply ashamed. The damage done to children in East Harlem is a shame to the patrons of the opera and the ladies and gentlemen dining at La Grenouille and so we embrace the idea of the safety net that catches the fallen, for which the wealthy pay a heavier share, because most Americans aren't willing to see shantytowns spring up outside town or have crowds of hollow-eyed children trailing us in the streets, keening and begging. Most Americans are not willing to let people die in a ditch or go hungry. Democrats aren't, that's for sure.

People are responsible for the dumb things they do, yes indeed. There is a Moment of Reckoning that comes occasionally to each one of us and we're entitled to it. The truth dawns. If you leave your bike outside it will rust. If you build on a flood plain, eventually you will get flooded out and your sofa be waterlogged and your linoleum come loose. If you're worried about drinking, stop. If you smoke cigarettes, you may wind up with lung cancer or emphysema. If you gamble, you may lose your shirt.

There are, however, broken people in this world and it does not help matters to order them to shape up and then walk away. You wouldn't do that with anyone you knew personally. Other people count, even broken ones. You cannot gallop through the streets like a Cossack and not notice who you are tromping into the dirt, who curses you as you go jangling past. You cannot do this in life, in business, or in politics, wielding power in behalf of your cronies in the American Petroleum Party—you really cannot—there will come a day of reckoning. You learn this when you're two years old and other little kids climb into the sandbox with you: the sand must be shared. Jesus said, "Unless ye become as little children, ye cannot enter into the kingdom of heaven."

8. Democrats are diehard teachers. Education is a heroic task and the answer to just about anything. The Peace Corps was pure Democratic idealism: send diligent young pedagogues out into the ramshackle parts of the world to teach hygiene and reading and corn planting and well digging and you will cast bread upon the waters and accomplish endless good. Offer college courses to prison inmates and you will raise morale and reduce violence in ways that lockdowns cannot. Sit the drug addicts down in a circle and get them to educate each other. Even violent young adolescent males can be rescued by the right sort of teacher. Education is an expensive proposition but there's no choice: nobody is born smart and we need good schools. Every child needs a beloved teacher in the early grades to instill a love of school, that enchanted world of books and paper and pencils and multiplication tables and maps and pictures, a love that will see the child through stretches of tedium and moments of panic. Every child needs teachers to idolize and imitate and around the snarly age of fourteen, when our daughters look at us with pained amusement and our sons with loathing, they need teachers who can channel their anger into social criticism and turn them into crusaders and satirists, as we once were, and then they will have children of their own and become us, the tedious authoritarians, and we will become beloved and eccentric grandparents, the genial revolutionaries, working secretly with our grandchildren against our common enemy, the parents. This is how the world turns. And teachers are crucial.

When you wage war on the public schools, you're attacking the mortar that holds the community together. You're not a conservative, you're a vandal. The sorehead vote is out there, the guys who have a few beers and wonder why the hell they should have to pay taxes for the schools when their kids have graduated, *What's the logic there, Joe?* and you can rouse them up and elect a school board to take revenge on the teachers and you do your community no favors.

Redneck used to refer to farmers like my uncle Jim

who did indeed have a red neck and forearms and face right up to the cap line on his forehead, but he was a generous sweet-tempered Christian man who lived out his faith. Now redneck just means somebody who'd happily spend $40,000 on a new pickup for himself and rise up in rage if someone asked him to pay $200 more for his kids' education. They're not farmers, they're just selfish bastards with shit for brains who only pay attention to education when they get pissed off. The school board, a dedicated bunch of hard-working underappreciated individuals, decides to change the school nickname from the Redskins to the Hornets, and the word goes out to the tavern dwellers and for the next school board meeting, the gymnasium is packed with furious large men venting their lifelong frustrations and in the fall the school board is thrown out of office and replaced by angry large people. That's redneck politics. The new school board sets about restoring Redskins honor, and trimming the budget, cutting out French and Spanish, establishing creationism as the prevailing science, cleansing the library of impurities, teaching faith-based social studies and history. High school becomes a forced hike down a long corridor of locked doors. You earmark your children for a career as drones—no need for them to learn a second language or write poetry or study physics: in a good redneck school, they only need to learn to sit quietly and recite the official patriotic liturgy and become angry rednecks like their daddies.

9. Democrats are realists. We care less about symbolism and enacting our own theology into law and making people listen to us intone a prayer (*O Thou who didst reveal Thyself to us, grant us victory over our despicable foes, and rain destruction and despair on them and cover their bodies with boils and sores, we do earnestly seek this in Our Savior's Name. Amen*) and we care more about the ordinary essentials of life. The New Deal put real people to work. My uncle Don was 18 in Wausau, Wisconsin, a big red-haired football star with no prospects, and got a job with the Civilian Conservation Corps and went off to build paths in national parks, a big experience for him. The Rural Electrification Act extended electric power to farms and villages that couldn't afford the capital investment: good old American socialism. The Keillor farm was one. They wired the barn so Uncle Jim had steady light to milk the cows by on winter mornings and a fluorescent light in the kitchen so he could read the Bible at night. Democrats brought about the school lunch program and the Public Health Service and integrated the armed forces, which then became a model of how Americans can be not so hung up on race. Democrats produced Head Start and food stamps and funded the college buildings to house the wave of boomers in the Seventies. The goal of Democrats has been to make this a nation of the middle class—educated people who own property and have a stake in the community and aren't easily bullied—and the most dramatic program was the GI Bill of Rights, which boosted a whole generation into the ranks of white-collar professionals.

We are all, God bless us, uniquely ordinary and rise up in the morning and wash our faces and pull our pants on and it would be nice to eat a breakfast that isn't full of poisons, send our children off to a good school, ride a safe bus to work at a building that complies with health laws, and use a cell phone that won't give us brain cancer. We'd like our employer to treat us fairly according to accepted practice. We'd like the police to guard the city against predators and vandals. We'd like to imagine that city officials are visionary and honest and committed to the common good and not in the pocket of the power company. We'd like to think that people in trouble get rescued. This is the Democratic view. We prefer the secular society to one in which persons of unpopular beliefs are ostracized, and we don't make the American flag into the Shroud of Turin, and we refuse to be cowed by our own government, and the sexual lives of our neighbors are not of profound interest. Republicans are troubled by homosexuality and can't figure out how not to think about it. Hunger and homelessness don't get their attention but the sight of two women kissing gets Republicans all buzzed, what a porch light does for moths. Democrats care more about health care and other staples of middle-class life. You drive out of St. Paul into the Republican suburbs and you see what the New Deal and Fair Deal and Great Society accomplished: they enabled people of modest means to get a leg up in the world and eventually become right-wing reactionaries and pretend that they sprang fully formed from their own ambitions with no help from anybody. And vote to deny to others what they themselves were freely given. Bless their hearts. But they're not Democrats.

10. The values of Democrats are rooted in courtesy and kindness. Everyone gets knocked around and failure is endemic and some get dealt a lousy hand and yet what gets us through the woods is the grace of God and the kindness of others, their small good deeds, unbidden, milk and honey. The American Indian didn't see much of our kindness, nor African Americans trying to pull themselves up out of sharecropper poverty, but for all our failings, there is a powerful river of mercy and understanding running through this nation's history and Democrats are in that stream.

Let not the sun set upon your wrath. Be grateful for your gifts. Say good morning. Let the customer have his say. Let aggravation pass without response. Yield to the car trying to cut in front of you. Float along in your unclouded brain and enjoy the passing parade. This is an old Democrat's advice.

Liberalism is the politics of kindness. It is all about opening the castle and letting the air in. Joseph McCarthy and the Red hunters of the Fifties were a visceral issue for liberals. Tailgunner Joe was an out-and-out bully and drunkard and liar who operated by innuendo and natural gas, a classic Republican prosecutor-politician, and he and his cohorts came afoul of a deep-seated American aversion to seeing people hauled up before a government committee to be grilled about their beliefs. We have the same aversion to homophobes: it's simply another form of cruelty.

This year, for the first time since Prohibition, it is proposed to mark up the Constitution in behalf of intolerance: the Republicans' Anti-Bruce & Larry Amendment, which everyone over the age of eleven knows will never be enacted—billions of lawyer hours would be spent trying to plumb the implications of the thing—it is only proposed because this President needs the votes of 7 or 8 million people who get the vapors if they see two men with earrings holding hands. It is purely a prize for the Christian right and the President's declaration for it was a brief statement, no questions, he was in and out like Speedy Gonzalez, wanting to deliver the goods without alarming anybody.

This old Democrat believes that your marriage is a matter between you and your spouse and its sanctity depends on the two of you. You can't beat each other and you can't cheat on each other, without the other having legal recourse, and otherwise you do not require state supervision. If the President wants to defend the sanctity of marriage, why not an amendment banning divorce?

Marriage in the United States shall consist only of the union of a man and a woman, or, in Utah, women. Neither this Constitution or the constutition of any State, nor state or federal law, shall be construed to permit divorce, except if the wife be found to have lost her virginity prior to marriage, in which case she shall be stoned. May not be applicable in Texas.

Gay marriage is an arguable issue and it will be argued. Some of us don't know what we think about it because it doesn't seem to touch us directly. We claim the right to be undecided. When Hallmark starts making cards for gay weddings, then we'll make up our minds.

Congratulations as you enter
Marriage to one of your own gender.
May the bells ring loud and gay
On your joyful wedding day.

I do think that if Larry loves Bruce and they go to the Church of the Blessed Whatever and the Rev. Starflower Moonbright intones some high-flown sentences and turns around three times and clicks his red slippers and proclaims them husband and husband, then I will wish them well and bring them a stainless-steel serving tray wrapped in nice silvery paper with a bow. This is the United States of America, 2004. It isn't Ireland, 1928. It isn't Iran. Odd and interesting things happen here. We should know this by now.

When I think of kindness, I think of my aunts, who looked out for neglected kids—runts and orphans and odd ducks, their specialty—and bestowed favors on them. They extended themselves to strangers. Their hearts went out to the lonely and the grieving. They did not let shyness get in the way of charity. They did not permit bullies to tromp around unimpeded; they spoke up. They abhorred cruelty. It offended them deeply. I don't suppose they would've "approved" of gay marriage but what if their nephew Larry and his partner Bruce were being shunned by some in the family and hounded by others and they had been met at the end of the driveway by Uncle Rex who told them to come no farther, the family Thanksgiving dinner was not open to them? What would my aunts have done? I suspect that one or two of them would've broken ranks and gotten in a car and chased down the prodigals and told them to come back and have some fatted turkey. That spirit runs deep in this country, I do believe. Great empires rise and fall, the famous come and go, cities boom and then languish, but kindness is a constant presence in America.

Chapter 12

* * ○ ○ ○ ○ ○ ○ ○ ○ ℗ ○ ○ ○ ○ ○ ○ ○ ○ * *

REPUBLICANS
I HAVE KNOWN

A bleeding heart liberal named John
Empathized hither and yon
And whenever he put
Down his small narrow foot,
He worried what he had stepped on.

I N THE fourth grade, I pored over a delicious book, *Runaway Home* by Elizabeth Coatsworth, about a family that moves from Maine to Washington State, traveling in a house trailer and having adventures along the way. I daydreamed that my family and I were nomads, migrating according to whim, camping in beautiful places and then moving on. (I think my dad had the same daydream.) I spent whole afternoons on the bank of the Mississippi, looking at the water flowing over the rapids, imagining myself on a boat heading downstream. I still think about it, standing on the landing in St. Paul and looking at the big curve of the river below downtown. I still love driving to the airport to get on a plane to wherever *A Prairie Home Companion* is playing that weekend. People tell me, "That must be hard on you, all that traveling," but it really isn't. You buckle up and rise to the skies and look at the patchwork quilt of farms pass beneath and feel loosened from the struggle of daily life.

The problem for a writer is that liberation from the struggle is tedious to write about: struggle is material for a writer and ease and comfort are not. And at 37,000 feet, a person starts to think like a Republican.

I didn't want to write a political book. A writer resists marching under a banner. A writer claims the freedom to sashay into whatever heretical notion takes his fancy. Writing is so risky to start with—you might spend three years pecking away at your novel and accomplish no more than if you had sat watching football on TV and eating Cheez-Its—so you cherish your freedom, the thing that makes writing fun, the chance to irritate and enrage.

Early in my career, I wrote stories for *The New Yorker* living in a rented house on a farm in Stearns County, working in a tiny bedroom on an Underwood typewriter on a desk made of a ¾-inch plywood slab set across two old filing cabinets, sat and tapped away for hours, looking out at the farmyard and old red barn and silo, and tried so hard to please New York that it queered my style and I had to go back to radio to learn to talk straight. Now I tell stories on the radio about Lake Wobegon and its God-fearing egalitarian inhabitants, and though I find grandeur in this, I feel that, at 61, I am still in search of what I was looking for when I was 18. What I really want is a long conversation with Grandpa and Grandma Denham who came over from Glasgow in 1906 with their six kids, Marion, Mary, Ruby, Margaret, Jean, and Bill, and settled into a big frame house on Longfellow Avenue. Grandpa was a railroad clerk who wore hightop black shoes and white shirts with silk armbands and spoke with a Scottish burr, so that *girls* came out "*gettles.*" He never drove a car or attended a movie or read a novel. I want to know why they came here, what they were looking for—the truth, not a children's fable—and if I have found it, maybe I can stop looking.

Maybe I just need to take up golf.

Maybe I should write a book about Republicans I have met and liked. Chet Atkins was a Republican and one of the finest human beings I ever met, a gentleman and artist and storyteller and a man with a true gift for friendship. I loved Chet, as so many people did, and there on his office wall hung pictures of him with Reagan, Bush the First, Lamar Alexander, everybody grinning. Senator Dave Durenberger once put an arm around me and wished me a Merry Christmas and told me to "just go on being who you are," after I had written a savage attack on a wretched despicable protégé of his. Years ago, when the National Endowment for the Arts was under attack over the Mapplethorpe pictures of naked men with things stuck in their orifices, I walked into the office of Senator Alan Simpson, the Republican whip, to make a case for the NEA and he couldn't wait to tell me about a game played by Wyoming cowboys in which you drop your trousers and try to pick up a quarter on a wooden bench using only your cheeks. A fine gentleman. Justice Harry Blackmun was a Republican of the old school, and showed me a framed photograph of himself and the rest of the Harvard Glee Club posing on the White House lawn with President Hoover. And a framed bullet that somebody shot through the window of his home, payment perhaps for his having written the majority opinion in *Roe v. Wade*. Every day, this modest man went for a walk after lunch at his office. He declined to take a security man along with him and followed the same route every day, returning to the Supreme Court building by the front entrance, often passing through a crowd of antiabortion picketers holding up pictures of dead embryos and not recognizing the slight bespectacled man in the overcoat who had done the devil's work.

I met President Reagan once back in 1991 with my stepdaughter, a film student at Columbia. Myself, I wouldn't know how to get an appointment with the mayor of Piscacadawadaquoddymoggin but the *New York Times* has clout and an editor there arranged it, hoping I'd write something sharp and satiric about the old man. We went to the top floor of a building in Century Plaza with a fine view of west LA and the ocean and in he came, beaming, though he hadn't a clue who we were or why we'd come. Had we had trouble finding the address? No. Were we enjoying LA? Yes. Had we visited the Reagan library? No. "But we got to see the old

Warner Brothers lot," Malene said. And that lit up the old man's eyes. He turned and bestowed his full sunny warmth on her. Nothing, it seemed to me, not a battalion of Young Republicans or a gold plaque from the National Rifle Association could have warmed his heart like a beautiful young woman who felt (she really did) that the Thirties were the heyday of moviemaking and who revered motion pictures starring old pals of his, and he got all twinkly and Irish. No wonder he got elected, despite his cranky view of the world and the canned quality of his every utterance, and was let off so easily for the Iran-Contra business, an impeachable offense if there ever was one.

I'd enjoy writing that book. And yet my life depends on the social compact that Republicans are determined to cripple by cutting taxes so as to starve government and kill off public services through insolvency and reduce us to a low-wage no-services plantation economy run by an enclave class that I do not wish to be part of. I don't want to move to a high-security building with a doorman and closed-circuit TV surveillance or a private suburban community with a guardhouse at the entrance and regular patrols by a private security force. I want to stay here in St. Paul where anyone can walk up to my front door, Jehovah's Witnesses or Boy Scouts selling Christmas wreaths or candidates for city council or firewood salesmen or cat burglars casing the joint, and I want the freedom to walk the streets and enjoy the civility of the city, and for that, the Republicans must be fought before their success destroys the neighborhood. When the coyotes become too numerous and bold, then in defense of small children you must go and deal with coyotes, whether you want to or not.

What bewilders me about Republicans is the coalition of the corporate Bourbon wing of the party and the Bible wing, two groups with little in common, but the Bible wing supplies the votes and the Bourbons take most of the booty. The Bourbons get tax cuts and deregulation and the Bibleists get a few vague gestures on symbolic issues such as gay marriage and school prayer. Like the Pharisees, the Bibleists enjoy public displays of religion. A roomful of movers and shakers gathered for a prayer breakfast that is all about bonding, backslapping, hobnobbing, and the prayers are read off 3x5 index cards, and there is a complete lack of heartfelt witnessing as you'd find among people of faith. At the prayer breakfast, if the Holy Spirit speaks, it is always in favor of tax cuts and less government regulation and preemptive military action. The Holy Spirit never comes out in favor of anything without clearing it with the Republican Party.

The Bibleists vow to put God back in the public schools, as if He were a small plaster icon and not the Creator of the universe. Evidently, when they hear public prayer, they sense the Spirit's presence. I don't. The public invocation (*O Thou Who didst turn water into wine, bless, we beseech Thee, this conference of the Water Sanitation Engineers of the North Central District . . .*) is a piece of sanctimonious boilerplate with the spiritual weight of a postage stamp. It has no connection to true prayer, the throwing of myself down in the presence of the Creator: *Lord have mercy, Lamb of God who takes away the sins of the world have mercy upon us. Our Father Who art in heaven, hallowed be Thy Name.* Saying the names of loved ones, putting myself wordlessly under God's wing. That is true prayer. Pharisee prayer is simply a political speech that is addressed to God, as if He needed instruction. Why are the Pharisees so willing to exploit the Christian faith for political mileage? They will have to answer that; I can't. But God is not mocked and does not find political cynicism appealing in any way.

Faith is private. It demonstrates itself in good works and love of neighbors but it doesn't need to puff up and blow a horn and bang on kitchen pans. Everyone must look in his own heart and ask, *Do I really believe or do I not?* Jews do this in the fall and Christians in early spring, during Lent. Most people do not believe. They have tried to believe and they wish they did believe and are sorry they don't, because they like to be around people who do, so they come to church, and enjoy the music and decor and the hallowedness of it all, but the faith is not in them. They don't need to tell me about it—they only need to answer to God on this matter. He will understand if the answer is no. He already knew that.

The tragedy is when people who don't believe are so tortured by their unbelief that they set out to scourge their fellow unbelievers. When you try to find the love of Christ at work in the Republican Party, it may take you awhile. The Christian Coalition was a Republican front with about as much to do with the Christian faith as the Elks Club has to do with large hoofed animals.

My parents said grace before every meal, with the plaster Brethren plaques on the wall—JESUS NEVER FAILS, and PRAYER CHANGES THINGS—and faithfully attended the breaking of bread on Sunday mornings and gospel meetings on Sunday nights and Bible readings on Wednesdays and patiently awaited the Rapture. The Brethren were gentle dissenters devoted to the Lord's Word who believed in separation from the things of the world. You shouldn't make big plans, or think too highly of yourself, or curry the favor of nonbelievers, or devote yourself to gathering wealth. They were deeply suspicious of earthly success. On Sunday morning you sat in the Brethren meeting hall, which was plain, unadorned, with no pictures or statues or gold or expensive things because the Brethren lived by the Word and didn't parade their Christian faith for effect. My father thought the baccalaureate "service" at the high school was silly on the face of it, mere religiosity, an attempt by the indifferent to play at religious ritual and thereby assuage their guilty conscience. And that's the Republican Party: its Christianity is about half fake because it scorns Jesus' command to love thy neighbor as thyself and it abuses any who take the commandment seriously. Better to be a principled atheist than a Christian for show. A man who employs the Lord as a special effect and makes a public performance of piety deadens his spiritual life and puts his own soul in danger.

America is not a religious country, no matter how many Americans say they believe in God. I've been in religious countries and this is not one of them. There is no Sabbath, no fasting or prohibitions, every day is a feast day. You can buy liquor on Sunday almost anywhere, find pornography in any Marriott or Wal-Mart, say any ugly, profane thing on the radio or anywhere—we're fat and sloppy and as disciplined as a battalion of cats, an impulsive, dreamy people walking around eating ice cream cones and eyeballing the girls' sweaters and dreaming of a big hit in the lottery. If God is looking for a nation to carry out His will on earth, it isn't this one. And it wasn't leftist professors who led us into the sins of the flesh: it was capitalist entrepreneurs. If the Pharisees really wanted to make this a God-fearing nation, they'd be taking up their cudgels against fellow Republicans.

Chapter 13

ARROGANCE

A progressive named Robert LaFollette
Said, "I don't care what you call it,
Social welfare, the dole,
Or a black hole,
I just want to get in your wallet."

DEMOCRATS are thought to be weak on foreign policy—fearful of the use of American power in the world—but what we fear is arrogance. History shows so clearly the stupidities of 1915—old men in power with little notion of where they were headed, afraid to betray uncertainty or fear, willing to sacrifice a generation of young men so that old men could parade around in their plumed helmets for a few more years—which was also the stupidity of Vietnam and is still with us today. Great harm has been done by strategists and theoreticians drawing lines on a map that represent real soldiers slogging through mud and mist toward impenetrable barriers that don't appear so on the map. The strategists draw the lines and issue the orders and have lunch in the officers' mess under the chandeliers and the soldiers move out into the rain and die in the desolate dark.

For my generation of college kids, travel to foreign places was a test of one's character and intelligence. We grew up curious about Europe and Asia and hoped to really experience it and not an Americanized version, to see villages with no Coca-Cola signs. We worked at marshaling a little French, some Italian, some German, as our humble offering to the natives so they might accept us.

When I lived in Denmark in the late Eighties, I went to parties and listened to the dinner speeches and songs and when the Dane sitting next to me asked, "Shall we speak English or Danish?" I said, "*Dansk, naturligvis. Vi er i danmark.*" And off I went down the slippery slopes. The Dane might be a reader of Updike and Cheever, but I chugged along in my patchy Danish, little shattered sentences stuck together with lumpy participles, because I wanted to get far away from arrogance and also because it's a unique pleasure to express your patriotism in a foreign tongue. You chatter in Danish about New York City and Graceland and LA and New Orleans, the magnificent West, Chicago, the redwoods, the Grand Canyon, all that Danes love about America, the mythological landscape of books and music. It isn't our politicians they admire.

When I lived there, Danes were still talking about the visit of Vice President Bush to speak at the Danish Fourth of July at Rebild Park in Jutland and how his armor-plated limousine had sunk down in the sand en route to the speaker's pavilion and how the man refused to get out of the damn car and walk 200 yards to the stage. He sat in his behemoth car with Old Glory flying from the front fender, surrounded by Secret Service, and it took twenty men on a hot day to push him and his tank through the sand to the pavilion where he disembarked and gave his speech on Freedom, America's Gift to the World. Denmark is a country where big shots walk. Mr. Bush made a big impression on the Danes.

I went to the Danish Fourth of July celebration in 1992 and the day before to a reception at the American ambassador's residence in Charlottenlund, a mansion with a swimming pool in back and a lawn big enough to play softball on. Thirty guests mingled in the sunshine, Danes from the ministry of education and various exchange programs and some Americans from the Embassy and a couple of Fulbrights, and then suddenly the Ambassador appeared, a beefy Republican with a big honk that made you flinch and look away, embarrassed that your country was represented by such a yahoo. He circulated through the crowd, grabbing people's shoulders ("Hey, how we doin' here? Need a refill?"), the perfect caricature of the self-made tycoon ("You want another beer? Hey! Go for it!"). The man represented the defeat of American satire. Mark Twain, H. L. Mencken, George Ade, Sinclair Lewis, and James Thurber had all beaten on this man for a hundred years and there wasn't a dent in him. He stood there, drink in hand, as fresh and happy and stupid as if *Babbitt* had never been written. He read his speech off a sheet of paper, bellowing into a microphone. "*Velkommen and Tak,*" he said. "And now I think I'll switch to English. Danish always sounds to me like someone choking on a potato." He paused for the laugh, not understanding that it's only funny if a Dane makes fun of Danish: coming from an American, it's rude. He read his little talk about the Fulbright program, said it was a good thing and he was in favor of it and stepped down, a Republican through and through, crass, smug, contemptuous of foreigners, inept at English, anti-intellectual and damn proud of it, and he got away with it because Danes admire America. Not for people like him but for jazz musicians, cartoonists, writers, and of course for the Americans who helped rescue Europe from the Nazis. He was a man writing a check on other people's accounts.

We Democrats do not want to be him. We prefer to stand with the tradition of Adams and Franklin and Jefferson, who made the voyage across the Atlantic and polished their French and learned to make their way by their wits and not by throwing money around or at the point of a cannon. America has produced great travelers and explorers and missionaries. They didn't stand behind a podium and thunder and threaten and strike a belligerent pose for domestic consumption, they went out into the world with courage and curiosity to take it on its own terms. They looked, they listened, they learned to walk lightly.

Chapter 14

9/11

A Republican lady of Knoxville
Bought her brassieres by the boxful,
Which she stuffed with corn kernels
And old Wall Street Journals
To keep the fronts of her frocks full.

I T HAS RAINED all morning on Republican and Democrat alike and at noon I go to the café. A soft and glittery world after rain. The urge to strive and accomplish and succeed relaxes on a rainy day. The chain gang is canceled, public hangings postponed. It's the day to savor the vast goodness of life. Once the water collects in rivers, men can fight over it and apportion it away from the gardens of the poor and lavish it on the fairways of the rich, but for now, it is simple socialism in the form of precipitation. Our neighbors' yard glistens, the dark brown patches where their three boys and our daughter have worn holes in the turf, scuffling around the swing set. I walk past Jim and Debra's house and the old Field house and turn the corner. A little girl died here two years ago. For weeks afterward, little bouquets of flowers were laid there and a little Styrofoam cross. There is tragedy that nobody can rescue you from. A thoughtless moment compounded by happenstance and a child is killed and you spend the rest of your life looking at the X and wondering why did it happen like that when it could have happened so many other ways. And on this same corner I once saw a bride and groom, just the two of them, in white and black, cross the street under an umbrella, heading for their reception at the University Club, in a downpour, he holding her hand up and forward, as if leading her in a dance.

I sit and drink coffee in the corner café on Selby and remember the Ten O'Clock Scholar near the U where I hung out forty years ago. Fishnet hung from the ceiling and candles burned in Chianti bottles and silent men played chess in the corner and sometimes a chick with a Swedish last name would sing the blues, *I'm going to town to get my ashes hauled because my good man he left me in the fall* and I sat in back, studying people, smirking at the ones who looked as if they might come from the horsey suburbs like Wayzata or North Oaks. The student art on the walls was all browns, ochre, black wash, shadowy, ominous, lonely figures, woodcuts, storm clouds, dark houses. Dark was cool and to be anguished meant you were serious.

I think if I sat here long enough, I might see my 18-year-old self walk in the door. He'd stand by the cash register and scan the room and his gaze would be merciless. I dread him looking at me. Here I am, walking softly into my sixties, a little astonished at my good fortune in life; when I was 18, I was poised on the crest of the hill, about to plunge down the slippery slope to a lifetime of failure. Nine years later, an unsolicited story of mine was bought by *The New Yorker* magazine and this stroke of good luck began to reverberate in my life. *The New Yorker* was a name that rang loud and long in the minds of midwesterners, and my association with the magazine was a powerful juju. I wrote a story for *The New Yorker* about the radio show *The Grand Ole Opry* at WSM in Nashville and that opened the door to my starting *A*

Prairie Home Companion in 1974. No commercial station would've been interested, and the classical music stations of public radio wouldn't have been either *but* there was that interesting item in my résumé, my connection to *The New Yorker* and that juju opened doors. It helped that my boss William H. Kling happened to harbor a secret affection for antique radio and of course it helped that I worked awfully hard (which one must do if one is not naturally gifted—as Grandma said, "What we lack in our heads, we must make up for with our feet") but looking back, I see that *The New Yorker*'s acceptance letter in the spring of 1969 was a magical coin dropped on my doorstep. So much happened to me as a result of that one thing—a minor *New Yorker* underling, riffling through boxes of stuff, came across my little story and snatched it up in her hand—and had she not, I'd be driving the Grand Avenue bus or waiting tables at the Lexington Café.

I always saw the radio show as a job, but one I do by reflex, so it doesn't depend on ambition or initiative or creativity. The Great Listener is standing over me, holding an old tennis ball, and as I look up at Him, panting, He throws the ball into the bushes and I tear after it and bring it back. I do that every week, over and over. I suffer over it as much as my mother dreaded knocking on doors to sell cookies but I am a lucky man. It goes back to when I hired an illegal alien to take care of my apartment, a handsome black-haired Tibetan woman whom I paid well, and she saved her money and brought her daughters to America from Nepal and they all became legal and moved to California, and on the morning she said goodbye, she held both my hands in hers, and she cried harder than anyone I ever said goodbye to, and she left a long white silk Buddhist prayer scarf tied to the door handle, and ever since then, I've had so much good fortune, I can't tell you.

I was a pale awkward boy of no great acumen, lost out on the periphery, and I managed to write myself into the center of things. I created a town and made myself the authority on it. I have been reckless, confused, sunk in misery, and squandered many chances. I have made sensible decisions that turned out to be stupendously dumb. But I love to go tearing off after the tennis ball on Saturday nights. Saturday is a long day of work, and then, at 5 P.M., the performance of *A Prairie Home Companion*, and afterward I get in my car and drive up the hill to home. A good day of work. Not so bad a deal, though when I look out the window and see Nathan Hale in the dark, contemplating his mortality, I do think about my own.

In July of 2001 I went down to the Mayo Clinic in Rochester and had an operation to sew up a leaky valve in my heart and by Labor Day I was on the road promoting a new novel. On September 10, 2001, I gave a reading at the Barnes & Noble bookstore on Union Square in New York City and around midnight, I sat with a few friends at a sidewalk café on 14th Street, the World Trade Center Towers shining in the night to the south of us, and enjoyed a big tray of Malpeque oysters and a Tanqueray martini. Eight hours later, it happened, the unthinkable, the black smoke and flame, the plane hitting the tower, the second plane banking into the second tower, the fireball, the buildings collapsing an hour later. I was up on West 90th Street and heard the first plane go over, heading down the Hudson at a desperately low altitude, and a few minutes later my phone rang and it was my friend Tony in the Village who had seen the fireball and was weeping.

It was, for a time, a catastrophe for which there was no name, there being no term for hijacking planes and crashing them into buildings, no single place name like Pearl Harbor, so people referred to it abstractly as *It* or "all of this," as in "Before all of this happened, we were thinking of going to Europe." Only after two or three months did people start to call it by its date, 9/11.

Like most New Yorkers, I kept putting myself in the place of the people on the planes: you take off from Boston and ascend through the cloud cover and about the time you get out your laptop, there's commotion up front and sounds of struggle and men going through the cockpit door and panic wells up in your chest and you say the Lord's Prayer and something tells you that the end has come and you will never see your children again and the silly argument with your wife about the Visa bill was your last conversation.

Or you're standing in the dining room on the 101st floor, picking up coffee and a bagel and cream cheese and dreading the conference about to begin which you were hoping not to attend, and there is a jolt that knocks plates off the table, and you think, *Earthquake,* and then there is smoke, and you dash to the stairwell, and it's full of smoke, and you sit on the floor and call 911 on your cell phone, and something in the voice of the woman at the other end tells you: that's it, Bud, it's over. Those people on the 101st floor started their day out here on the streets with the rest of us.

All that week, we heard stories of men and women in the towers who, in a horrible moment, stifled their fear and looked out for others. All week, New Yorkers went about their business quietly, thoughtfully—no horns honking, no cursing and flipping the bird, none of the usual smart-ass stuff—and on Friday, there was a twilight vigil all over the city. People stood on the sidewalk holding candles, in front of brownstones and luxury co-ops and public housing projects and on street corners, some of them singing "My Country 'Tis of Thee" and "America the Beautiful" and "Amazing Grace." I stood with a bunch on West 90th and then I walked around the Upper West Side and saw little groups of old lefties and diehard liberals standing on sidewalks holding candles and singing about the fruited plains and spacious skies, the thoroughfare of freedom across the wilderness, and *O beautiful for patriot's dream that sees beyond the years; thine alabaster cities gleam undimm'd by human tears* and sang it with tears in their eyes in the midst of the shining city that was the dream of so many immigrant patriots. A little knot of singers in front of each building, New Yorkers in communion—*Who organized this? Whose idea was it?* I didn't know but at the moment it seemed almost spontaneous.

Such a rare moment in New York and so fervent, its message one of simple communalism: *we are all here together.* Along with the pages and pages of obituaries in the *Times* it was the most moving aspect of the week after 9/11—the spirit of New Yorkers silently rallying to each other. It reminded me of my first clear experience of New York, when Dad brought me to the city in August 1953. I was 11. He came to visit some friends in Brooklyn whom he'd met when he was stationed at the Army Post Office near Times Square during the war. We stayed with them in their little apartment in Brooklyn. One hot night, unable to sleep, Dad and I went for a walk and stopped at a candy store and got a couple sodas and stood on the curb and drank them. Across the street was a park, a square really, a block long on each side, with trees and grass, park benches around the perimeter facing the sidewalk. The park was full of people sleeping on blankets. Families curled up together on the grass, asleep. Not hoboes: families, escaping from hot apartments to the cool outdoors, sleeping in a little island of dark in the middle of the great shining city, and on the park benches sat men, smoking, talking in low voices. Dad and I stood and looked at them and nothing was said but that picture of nocturnal encampment became a permanent memory of the city, along with Ebbets Field, Coney Island, push-cart peddlers, the Empire State Building, and the Staten Island ferry.

It was the worst of times and the best of times. The event drove out trash TV for a week or so, and all the lazy cynicism of the young, and talk radio started talking about something real. (There was a tone of maudlin self-absorption that crept in gradually, and on the first anniversary of 9/11 National Public Radio broadcast two hours of claptrap, a couple dozen overwrought navel-gazers calling in to share their *feelings* about 9/11 and how it, like, meant for them, you know, like, the loss of innocence or something, people who had lost no-body in the disaster, hadn't been within a hundred miles of it, but nonetheless had *feelings* to share. It made you want to poison their fish tank.) Down in the Village, closed to motor vehicles, people walked in the streets, dust and smoke still hanging in the air but restaurants were open, even sidewalk cafés, people making heroic attempts at normal life, trying to enjoy a glass of wine and a bowl of steamed mussels and talk about the kids and movies and jobs and only mention in passing the horror and destruction a couple miles away—*Do you think they'll find survivors in the rubble?* No, I doubt it.—What a city. Hit with terrible force and two days later people were attending movies again. Down near Trinity Church and Wall Street and the Woolworth Building, heartbreaking devastation, thousands of bodies, exhausted police and firemen, and all over the city, people in grief and shock, and yet classical musicians made the long trek down to St. Paul's Chapel a few hundred feet from the rubble of the Towers and played Mozart and Bach and Haydn for the salvage workers taking a coffee break. Evil had struck us, but life went on and we accepted it as a gift. There is no closure, no resolution, we simply go on.

Who could have guessed in those quiet anguished days in New York the political rewards that the Republicans would reap from all those deaths? How George W. Bush, who has never accepted the slightest responsibility for 9/11 though there is mounting evidence that he had been warned in quite specific terms in the months prior, so smartly stood amid the smoking rubble and spoke into a bullhorn and, back in Washington, snatched at a Democrat's idea for a security superagency and set out to create an immense new bureaucracy to paper over the mistakes of immense old bureaucracies and an ad agency came up with the weird name, Homeland Security, a word Americans have never used to refer to the U.S.A., a word you'd expect to hear spoken in a war movie by a man with a monocle flicking his riding crop against his shiny black boots, a new Achtung Department to put out warnings and recommend duct tape to seal doors and windows and caches of bottled water and dried fruit in the basement, and he suckered some Democrats into opposing his Achtung bill on grounds it violated civil liberties and also stripped government workers of certain rights, whereupon he wrapped the flag around himself in the 2002 election and played patriotism like a $29 accordion and portrayed Democrats as Al Qaeda sympathizers and then, postelection, launched a war against Iraq which had exactly nothing to do with 9/11 that anyone knew of, and made plans to hold the 2004 Republican convention in New York to capitalize on the tragedy, which he has exploited as the Defining Moment of his Presidency and used to squelch dissent and render the press supine and soften up the opposition to his right-wing judicial appointments and his gutting of the regulatory agencies, all of which would have been anathema to most of the people who died in the Towers. Some of them were Republicans, true, but New York Republicans are a lot closer to Democrats than they are to George W. Bush.

That is the stink drifting through this election year. The New Yorkers and Jerseyites who died in the collapse of the Towers and what this shallow and hard-shelled man failed to do for them that he had sworn to do and how he stood on their graves and gave a sermon diametrically opposite to what they believed. It isn't the Florida recount or the Supreme Court decision. No, it's 9/11 that we keep coming back to. It wasn't the "end of innocence," or a turning point in our history, or a cosmic occurrence, it was an event, a lapse of security, and patriotism shouldn't prevent people from asking hard questions of the man who was purportedly in charge of national security at the time.

The men and women who rode the elevators up to work that morning came in on PATH trains from New

Jersey or rode in on the Long Island Rail Road and then took the subway down to the WTC or they rode the Lexington Avenue subway down to City Hall and maybe walked across City Hall park behind the Boss Tweed building and the Woolworth tower. I used to have an office in the Woolworth. I remember the neighborhood. The crowds of suits heading to work, the bike messengers, the Wall Street crowd. There was a lunchwagon on the street with an Arab guy in it where I stopped for a cup of coffee and a bagel every morning, and after two mornings, he knew that I wanted a large coffee with milk and a poppyseed bagel with cream cheese and scallions. *After two mornings he knew this.* Now that's what you call free enterprise.

Those men and women were part of a world utterly different from that of George W. Bush's Texas. They belonged to a world of theater and books and street life and freedom of thought and the democracy of the subway. They deserve better than to be the platform for intolerance and the demolition of social services and handing out bonuses to the rich.

Whenever I think of those New Yorkers hurrying

along Park Place or getting off the No. 1 Broadway local, hustling toward their office on the 90th floor, the morning paper under their arms, and then I think of that non-reader George W. Bush and how he hopes to exploit those people and with a little economic uptick, maybe the capture of Osama, some good TV ads, cruise to victory in November and proceed to get some serious nation-changing done in his second term, I feel a little warm behind the eyebrows.

But I refuse to be furious. I am a happy Democrat living in a great country, at home in St. Paul, Minnesota, where no matter what, there is a lot of satisfaction going on a good deal of the time. Complaint is a cherished art form, here as in New York, but the streets of St. Paul are clean, the cops and firemen are the finest in the land, the parks are lovely, the old Victorian houses are cherished, and the new Italian restaurant three blocks from here, the one with the shady patio and the terrific risotto, is thriving mightily. The social compact is still intact, knock on wood. Life is pretty good in St. Paul. Call it apathy, but really it's satisfaction. Or poise. As Whitman wrote—

Me imperturbe, standing at ease in Nature,
Master of all, or mistress of all—aplomb in the
    midst of irrational things,
Imbued as they—passive, receptive, silent as they,
Finding my occupation, poverty, notoriety, foibles,
    crimes, less important than I thought;
O to be self-balanced for contingencies!
O to confront night, storms, hunger, ridicule,
    accidents, rebuffs, as the trees and animals do.

When I was young I was more perturbed by irrational things and loved the insurrectionist swashbuckling aspect of politics, the forces of Reason storming the Bastille, the good peasants baring their butts at the Blanc Palais, the king's courtiers mincing and fawning on *Meet the Press*, the royal artillery barrage of TV commercials, the ferocity of the peasants' attack on the Royal Flank, the shudder and screech as the regime collapsed in 1968 and again in 1974—it was all terribly gratifying back then in my trumpet days. I'm older now and mellower, and prefer the tuba. Richard M. Nixon had his points: he went to China, he got the cleanup of the Great Lakes under way, he put Harry Blackmun on the Supreme Court. Lyndon B. Johnson was revealed in the transcripts of his long anguished telephone calls to colleagues, a different LBJ from the one we loved to despise back then; he was a man in despair over Vietnam who saw all too clearly the cataract he was being swept toward, that dreadful and wasteful war that poisoned our politics and slaughtered hundreds of thousands of people because Democrats were afraid of being called "weak on communism" and so the ship got on the reef and we didn't know how to reverse the engines.

You go to the Vietnam Memorial in Washington today and look at the names on the Wall, you feel united with the folks around you, the families still in grief for boys long gone, the old vets, the schoolkids. All the political divisions that tore us up thirty years ago don't seem so important now compared to the loss of those lives. There is a feeling of solidarity that you also get at the Lincoln Memorial and Ellis Island and Gettysburg.

Someday the Vietnam War will mean no more to people than the War of 1812 and the Wall will be something to lean against as you eat lunch and look at the girls and plan your weekend; I pray there will not be some new memorial to the dead of some new horror.

Most people treasure the sense of true national unity, which we briefly had after 9/11 until the Republicans took out a trademark on the tragedy—the sense of unity we try to relight every Memorial Day. (The Fourth of July is gone, a big dead hollow holiday, but Memorial Day retains a little of its spirit.) I feel that American solidarity sometimes when listening to jazz, especially Armstrong and Ellington and Benny Goodman, the old guys who swept Europe and whose music was a living symbol to the Resistance of all that was worth dying for in the fight against Hitler. I feel it sometimes on my way out of the theater after a terrific performance of a great musical, *Gypsy* or *The Music Man* or *Oklahoma!*—the American musical, a peculiar construction whose success depends on ensemble, not celebrity, and you sometimes see a student or amateur production that simply *works* and *sweeps you away* and it's exhilarating (to an American anyway), all those shining faces, like seeing your kid's baseball team play *over its head* for nine solid innings, and all of us Americans walk out of the theater feeling unaccountably joyful together. I feel it sometimes at the ballpark, sometimes reading the glory that is American poetry, feel it driving a car across Wyoming or through the Civil War battlefields of Virginia, Chancellorsville and the Wilderness and Fredericksburg and Antietam, or along the Mississippi. I wish that Republicans had a little more genuine love of this country and weren't still hung up on the Sixties and so medieval in their worship of rank and hierarchy. They slid into Washington on an oil slick like a gang of small-time mafiosi and sold out representative democracy to their special patrons and backers and corrupted a lot of good Christian people in the process. This year, as in the past, they will portray us Democrats as embittered academics, desiccated Unitarians, wacked-out hippies and communards, people who talk to telephone poles, the party of the Deadheads. They will wave enormous flags and show over and over the footage of firemen in the wreckage of the World Trade Center and bodies being carried out and they will lie about their economic policies with astonishing enthusiasm. They denounce government as if it had only repressed them and civilization frustrated their noblest instincts, to which I say: "Wyoming. Go there. Try western North Dakota." Go find a tanktown on the old N.P. line and wrest your living from the dry soil and be as paranoid and angry as you like. It's a big country; the principles of Republicans may work very well on a 5000-acre ranch. But you can't run cities that way and cities are where most people live.

Dante said that the hottest place in hell is reserved for those who in time of crisis remain neutral, so I have spoken my piece, and thank you, dear reader. It's a beautiful world, rain or shine, and there is more to life than winning. The thing that has been is the thing that shall be; and the thing that is done is that which shall be done: there is nothing new under the sun. And the race is not to the swift nor the battle to the strong nor riches to men of understanding, but time and chance happeneth to them all. Lord, have mercy.

As soon as I finish this book, I am going to walk around the block for a cup of coffee and watch the parade go by on Selby Avenue, sit at ease, passive, receptive, silent, in the midst of this irrational election, like a horse in a rainshower, like a tree, like an old bird on the branch, unperturbed. If you see me, come sit down, there is more to talk about.